Ruth Soukup is equal parts fierce,
is the real deal. She has experien
and has wisdom to share. When y
equipped to start tackling your big

MW01032135

HAL ELROD, author of *The Miracle
Morning* and *The Miracle Equation*

Ruth Soukup is the real deal. She's one of the smartest, bravest, and
kindest people I know. *Do It Scared* is packed with truth and insight. If
you want to overcome the fear holding you back, use this book as a guide.
I promise, it will be life-changing!

LISA LEONARD, jewelry designer and author of *Brave Love*

If you're tired of playing small and are ready to embrace your future, Ruth
Soukup offers the actionable steps you need to get started. *Do It Scared*
is a practical guide to identifying your limiting beliefs, overcoming your
fears, and creating the life you've dreamed of.

MICHAEL HYATT, *New York Times* bestselling author

Ruth Soukup is a bold, brave hero in this world. Her story, strength, and
rare ability to see the world from a lens of truth and possibility make
her one of the most inspiring people I've ever met. *Do It Scared* is the
ultimate book for our generation, which needs practical tools for self-
reliance more than ever before.

SUSIE MOORE, confidence coach and author

People love to dream, imagine, and hope. But then fear pops up, and those
dreams get stuck in the mire of regret and inaction. *Do It Scared* will
move you from crippling fear to a life of purpose and meaning, evidenced
by physical, emotional, spiritual, and relational abundance. Get ready
to move from "I wish" to "I did."

DAN MILLER, *New York Times* bestselling
author of *48 Days to the Work You Love*

This brilliant book is a road map for turning big thoughts into big things.
Ruth Soukup helps you understand the root of your fears so you can
choose courageous action instead of fear-ridden reaction. "Do it scared"
is more than a catchphrase; it's a bold action plan to help you get out of
your own way so you can get where you want to go.

TESS MASTERS, author of *The Blender Girl* and *The Perfect Blend*

Do It Scared came at a time in my life when I felt worn down, weary, and paralyzed on what steps to take to move forward in my career. It gave me the encouragement I needed, while arming me with tools for making an action plan to get back in the game.

ERIN ODOM, author of *More Than Just Making It* and creator of thehumbledhomemaker.com

Finally a book that doesn't make fear the enemy but instead channels it as a powerful resource to achieve what you want! My only fear now is that you won't read this book.

MIKE MICHALOWICZ, author of *Clockwork* and *Profit First*

Do It Scared is required reading for anyone needing to overcome the fears they face to achieve a life they love. This is not some gimmicky, feel-good, self-help book. With more than four thousand people surveyed and researchers hired to analyze the data, this enlightening book shows us how to get past our fear in a way that is inspiring and not shaming.

BRI MCKOY, author of *Come & Eat*

Do It Scared systematically disarms the fear that holds so many hostage and keeps them from reaching their God-given potential.

BOB LOTICH, author of *Managing Money God's Way*

If you ever find yourself saying, *I'll never succeed at this*, you must read this book. *Do It Scared* opened my eyes to all the ways I allow fear to cripple my possibilities. Ruth Soukup offers practical strategies for overcoming fears and invites us to take hold of the success we were designed to achieve.

BECKY KOPITZKE, author of *The Cranky Mom Fix* and *Generous Love*

When Ruth Soukup shares her wisdom on goal setting and dreaming big, I take note. "Do it scared" may have started as her mantra, but I've watched her implement the tools and encouragement detailed in this highly recommended handbook, and no one does it better.

JEN SCHMIDT, speaker and bestselling author of *Just Open the Door*

Ruth Soukup understands what it's like to overcome the hard things that can hold us back. I highly recommend this practical, encouraging, and introspective approach to overcoming fear and living the life you've always dreamed of!

RUTH SCHWENK, founder of TheBetterMom.com and coauthor of *Pressing Pause*

Do It Scared is the perfect resource for those who are tired of being imprisoned by fear. If you are ready to confront fear head on and live the life you were meant to, this book is a must-read.

MIKE AND CARLIE KERCHEVAL, cofounders of FulfillingYourVows.com and bestselling authors of *Consecrated Conversations*

Ruth Soukup knows how to ignite a flame that burns in the face of fear! If inner alarms prevent you from pursuing your dreams, *Do It Scared* can be your go-to guide, just as it has been mine.

RACHEL WOJO, author of *One More Step*

Reading about the fear archetypes helped me better understand what's holding me back and also empowered me with specific ways to overcome my fears. I absolutely loved it.

JOANN CROHN, founder of No Guilt Mom

I struggle with the fear of losing balance, which will lead to failure. Yet I was convicted after reading this line from *Do It Scared*: "We're not called to balance; we're called to purpose." Ruth teaches that whatever we put our efforts toward has a purpose. This book can help you move past your fears and achieve the purpose for which you were designed.

KATE AHL, owner and CEO of Simple Pin Media

Ruth Soukup has given us an authentic, brilliant, and practical guide to creating a life we love. *Do It Scared* imparts tools and techniques so we can discover our fears and find the courage to push through them. Ruth's vulnerability about her fears and how she has still created a life she loves is so inspiring!

NICOLE RULE, owner of greatestworth.com and mentee of Ruth Soukup

Ruth Soukup helps you recognize the way your fears manifest themselves through her seven fear archetypes, shows you how to internalize principles of courage that can spur you on as you conquer your fears, and shares practical strategies for breaking down those goals into manageable daily action steps so you can show up and succeed every day.

ABBY LAWSON, author and owner of justagirlandherblog.com and abbyorganizes.com

Do It Scared is an essential read for every woman who has ever felt they aren't living to their full potential because something has held them back. Inspiring, informative, and truly enlightening.

CHRISSY HALTON, owner of OrganiseMyHouse.com

"Do it scared" is my new mantra. I hate letting fear hold me back, and this book gives me permission to acknowledge these fears so I can get past them. Ruth Soukup gives powerful advice and insights both from her own personal experiences and from the stories of the lives she has changed.

SAIRA PERL, founder of MomResource.com

Raw, real, and powerful! *Do It Scared* is a compelling reminder of what's possible when we push past our comfort zone and get out of our own way. If you need a kick in the pants to keep going, this is a must-read.

ABBY RIKE (abbyrike.com), author of *Working It Out*

I've dealt with fear my entire life, and reading *Do It Scared* opened my eyes and empowered me to move beyond the places where I've been stuck. Ruth's ability to break down a manageable action plan and speak truth to eliminate excuses provides invaluable tools to apply to our lives.

KASEY TRENUM, founder of kaseytrenum.com

Do It Scared took me through a personal therapy session, gave me self-awareness, and had me winning a championship game all at the same time. This book gave me words to understand my fear and practical steps to walk it out and turn it into a positive. I now know how to swap my fear out with courage, and it feels liberating.

TAI MCNEELY, cofounder of His and Her Money

Do It Scared is a refreshing and unique read that helped me see both my strengths and my weaknesses in a new and positive light while equipping me to finally get over the roadblocks that have kept me from achieving my biggest goals.

JENNIFER ROSKAMP, founder of The Intentional Mom

Do It Scared is a book every woman needs to read. Not only does the book help you dig up the root cause of your fear, but Ruth also doses out the perfect blend of empathy mixed with tough love and encouragement. I'm recommending this read to all of my friends.

TANIA TAYLOR GRIFFIS, blogger at www.runtoradiance.com

Do It Scared is a gift to women who want to live a courageously full life but don't know how. Ruth practices what she preaches, so her advice is not only incredibly inspiring but actionable. She is the encouraging mentor every woman needs in her life.

TASHA AGRUSO, founder and CEO of Kaleidoscope Living

What is the number one thing stopping you from becoming the woman you were born to be? Fear. *Do It Scared* is the primer you need to finally look fear in the face forever. Do it scared, and then do it all.

CLAIRE DIAZ-ORTIZ, author and speaker, ClaireDiazOrtiz.com

I can think of almost nothing more important than stepping forward, facing our fears, and doing what scares us most. Ruth Soukup gives brilliant insights into what holds us back and, most importantly, how to overcome challenges and "do it scared." If you want to live your greatest life and truly shine bright, I can't recommend her book enough!

MICHAEL SANDLER, host of the *Inspire Nation Show*
(www.InspireNationShow.com)

Do It Scared helps you drop all your silly excuses and do it scared, so you can actually live the life you want and deserve. Ruth Soukup is the coach every woman needs in her corner.

GRY SINDING, entrepreneur, business trainer, strategist, and motivational speaker

We've all faced our own battles, and Ruth Soukup's courage is a testament to the incredible power of embracing your story and sharing it with the world. She reminds us that even if we're terrified, even if we aren't experts, even if we feel broken inside, we are capable and deserving of an abundant life and worthy of love.

CATHY HELLER, songwriter and host of the *Don't Keep Your Day Job* podcast

I'm amazed at how Ruth Soukup is able to pinpoint our insecurities, fears, and limiting beliefs; hold up a mirror to them; and then provide a plan to overcome the things holding us back. Everyone should read this book at least once a year to help them remember exactly who they are and what they can do if they "do it scared."

KIM ANDERSON, blogger and author of *Live, Save, Spend, Repeat*

As an outcast archetype, I can relate to so much of what Ruth Soukup highlights in this amazing book. I'm a huge fan of finding the courage to operate just outside of your comfort zone—that's where all the magic happens! This book is full of actionable tips on how to move through the hard times.

ABBY WALKER, CEO of Vivian Lou and author of *Strap on a Pair*

Watching Ruth Soukup face her fears and "do it scared" has inspired me to do the same. Life is too short to live any other way, and this is the perfect book for anyone who wants to live a life of joyfully overcoming their fears and achieving things they never thought possible.

RACHEL HOLLAND, blogger at SurvivingTheStores.com and HowToHomeschoolForFree.com and essential oil educator at TheOILnation.com

Do It Scared helped me embrace the procrastinator attribute and change it to a strength. I've already seen improvements in my business and in my personal life.

JENNIFER DURSTELER, physician assistant and owner of Deja Vu Med Spa, Goodyear, Arizona

Do It Scared is the book I wish I had read ten years ago, because I would have reached my goals so much faster. This is the kind of book that does so much more than sit on the shelf. You can't help but take action after you've read it.

LAURA SMITH, founder of I Heart Planners

do it
scared™

FINDING THE COURAGE
TO FACE YOUR FEARS,
OVERCOME ADVERSITY, AND
CREATE A LIFE YOU LOVE

Ruth Soukup

*To my amazing, incredible,
freakishly enthusiastic team
at Ruth Soukup Omnimedia—
this book is as much a result
of your hard work as it is mine*

ZONDERVAN

Do It Scared
Copyright © 2019 by Ruth Soukup

Requests for information should be addressed to:
Zondervan, *3900 Sparks Dr. SE, Grand Rapids, Michigan 49546*

ISBN 978-0-310-35381-2 (hardcover)

ISBN 978-0-310-35384-3 (international trade paper edition)

ISBN 978-0-310-35383-6 (audio)

ISBN 978-0-310-35382-9 (ebook)

Any internet addresses (websites, blogs, etc.) and telephone numbers in this book are offered as a resource. They are not intended in any way to be or imply an endorsement by Zondervan, nor does Zondervan vouch for the content of these sites and numbers for the life of this book.

Published in association with the literary agency of Wolgemuth & Associates, Inc.

Cover design: Melissa Poe
Cover photography: Nick Davis
Interior design: Kait Lamphere

Printed in the United States of America

19 20 21 22 23 24 25 /LSC/ 15 14 13 12 11 10 9 8 7 6 5 4 3 2 1

contents

Invisible Chains 11

PART 1: THE FEAR ARCHETYPES

1. The Procrastinator 21
   When you're most afraid of making a mistake
2. The Rule Follower 30
   When you're most afraid of coloring outside the lines
3. The People Pleaser 40
   When you're most afraid of what other people will think
4. The Outcast 50
   When you're most afraid of rejection
5. The Self-Doubter 61
   When you're most afraid that you're not enough
6. The Excuse Maker 72
   When you're most afraid of taking responsibility
7. The Pessimist 83
   When you're most afraid of adversity

The Fear Archetypes at a Glance. 94

PART 2: THE PRINCIPLES OF COURAGE

8. Dare to Think Big 99
   *Because stretch goals are the secret to getting
   and staying motivated*
9. Rules Are for Suckers 109
   Because you should never be afraid to think for yourself

10. Always Own It 118
   Because you are in complete control of the choices you make

11. Embrace Honest Feedback 127
   Because everyone needs true accountability

12. There Are No Mistakes, Only Lessons 134
   Because every breakdown leads to a breakthrough

13. Balance Is Overrated. 141
   Because if everything is important, nothing is

14. Just Keep Going 151
   Because nothing will ever take the place of persistence

The Principles of Courage at a Glance. 161

PART 3: COURAGE IN ACTION

15. Claim Your Target. 165
   If you aim at nothing, you'll hit it every time

16. Find Your *Why* 174
   Your why *must be bigger than your fear*

17. Create Your Action Plan 183
   Break down your big goals into manageable bites

18. Form Your Own Truth Club. 194
   Surround yourself with people who will make you better

19. Stop Comparing 204
   Create the life you love, not the life someone else wants

20. Eliminate Excuses. 212
   Stop giving yourself a way out, and instead push through

21. Stay Encouraged 223
   Take the time to celebrate your wins along the way

Courage in Action at a Glance. 234

Acknowledgments 237
Notes 239

invisible chains

Fear is a funny thing.

It's one of our most basic human instincts, intended to protect us from all those dangers that might cause us harm and to jolt us to action when a threat becomes imminent. Our fear is designed to save us, and, interestingly enough, a lack of fear in perilous situations could actually be a sign of mental illness. We're *supposed* to be scared.

And yet that same fear can also be an invisible chain that ties us down and keeps us stuck. Instead of keeping us safe, it paralyzes us and prevents us from moving forward, from taking risks or putting ourselves out there, from having the courage to follow our dreams and create a life we love.

The very instinct designed to protect us also holds us back.

And oh, does it ever! Believe me, I know.

You see, fear has been a very real and active part of my life for as long as I can remember. I'm scared of heights and of looking like a fool. I get nervous in big crowds, and I'm terrified of small talk. I'm always afraid people aren't going to like me, or that they'll think I'm annoying or weird or not worth their time. I hate putting myself out there or being vulnerable. I'm scared of failing or making a mistake, and what that might say about me. And not too long ago, just the thought of having to speak to a crowd was enough to give me a panic attack.

All that fear was standing in my way, just like it does for so many others.

Wendy has always wanted to own her own bakery and coffee shop, but it just seems so daunting. In fact, she is so terrified she might fail that she turned down a generous offer from a generous investor that would have provided her with both the capital and the training she needed to get started.

Kyra was a talented dancer who spent years studying ballet but let her intense fear of rejection stop her from auditioning for a professional dance company, even though that had been her goal all along. Years later, she still feels like she missed out on achieving her full potential.

Trina doesn't want to practice law anymore. For years she has wanted to leave her dad's law firm to start her own business, but she is terrified of letting him down. She feels burdened by the weight of this responsibility and by the sadness of not being able to do her own thing.

Nancy wants to travel. She dreams about just getting in her car and driving all over the fifty states and Canada and then venturing even farther from there. But it just feels too risky for a single sixty-year-old woman to do by herself, and deep down, she doesn't know if she has it in her.

Liv is a scientist, which means a big part of her job is writing journal articles, but she is often afraid to share her writing with anyone before she has perfected it. She's always worried that she'll appear incompetent, or that someone will think she's not qualified. She knows it's not rational, but that fear is always there.

The same story plays out in a million different ways every day.

A big dream. An even bigger fear. And then, inevitably, a huge regret.

But it doesn't have to be this way.

Several years ago, I made a decision for myself that changed everything.

I decided to stop letting fear stand in my way.

I realized it was okay to be afraid—that everyone is afraid sometimes—but that it wasn't okay to let fear prevent me from doing all those things I really wanted to do. I realized I needed to figure out a way to leverage fear to my advantage.

So I decided that from then on, I would just *do it scared*.

Do it scared became my mantra, a little phrase I repeated to myself every time I felt nervous or afraid, every time I stepped outside of my comfort zone or took a risk or felt unsure of myself. Which, let's be honest, was pretty much all the time.

Once I became an entrepreneur, the Do It Scared mantra became the first of my company's fundamental core values, and eventually it became a rallying cry for the members of our communities at both Living Well Spending Less® and Elite Blog Academy®, so much so that I was inspired to start the *Do It Scared with Ruth Soukup* podcast to help others—and myself—face our fears, overcome obstacles, and, most importantly, create a life we *love*.

You might even say I became a little obsessed.

And that's where this book comes in.

THE FEAR ARCHETYPES™

Over the past nine years, as I navigated my own fears and talked with many members of our communities, I began to recognize just how big of an impact fear has on our lives—especially for women.

It's devastating to hear so many people in our community say they feel like they're sitting on the sidelines of their own life, afraid to go all in, terrified of making a mistake, of letting people down, of failing, or of being laughed at. They see the things they'd like to do and yet don't, simply because they're too afraid.

But as I talked to more and more women about this topic, I also started to realize that not all fear is created equal. Oh, don't get me wrong, we're all afraid of something. We all have fear, and we're all impacted by fear in some way, but the way fear manifests itself in our lives varies greatly. One person fears failure, while another fears rejection. One person fears being held responsible, while another is paralyzed at the thought of getting it wrong, whatever "it" may be.

I decided I wanted to go deeper, and boy, did I ever! I surveyed more than four thousand people in my communities about the role of fear in their lives and then hired a team of researchers to help me analyze a staggering amount of data. I was particularly interested in finding out more about how fear holds us back from pursuing our dreams, reaching our goals, and chasing opportunities.

The survey asked questions about goals and life satisfaction, as well as questions about experiences of fear and adversity—about times when fear had stopped someone from pursuing a goal or a dream, and about times when someone had pushed through fear in order to accomplish something. Several of the questions were open-ended, and the stories people shared about their experiences ran the gamut from completely inspiring to utterly heartbreaking. Many of these stories are represented throughout this book, either as quotes from survey responses or as slightly modified stories and archetype personas.

The survey results were incredibly insightful in several ways, but one discovery stood out above all the others. In fact, the moment it clicked into place, it nearly took my breath away. What's more, it made sense of so many confusing and unanswered questions. That aha moment was the discovery of seven fear patterns—seven distinct ways fear plays out in our lives, specifically in the way it impacts our willingness to step outside of our comfort zones to pursue a dream or opportunity. And because I like naming things (an obsession my team will readily attest to), I call these seven patterns "fear archetypes." They include the Procrastinator, the Rule Follower, the People Pleaser, the Outcast, the Self-Doubter, the Excuse Maker, and the Pessimist.

And that's where it *really* gets fascinating. Because, you see, while each of us possesses a few qualities of all seven archetypes, most of us have at least one dominant archetype that affects us more strongly than the others and plays out in our lives in more noticeable ways. Like fear itself, each of the seven archetypes has both negative and positive qualities—traits that can either hinder us or help us.

The fact that everyone experiences fear differently means that the path to *overcoming* fear will also be a little bit different for everyone. Thus, knowing the specific way that our fear plays out— our fear archetype—is essential to knowing exactly how to move past that fear.

THE DO IT SCARED FEAR ASSESSMENT™

Understanding the unique and specific ways in which fear might be holding you back is a critical first step in being able to overcome that fear. Even so, it's not always easy to identify those specific qualities in ourselves. To assist you in this process, my team and I created an online fear assessment that will help you identify your specific fear archetype, which you can access at doitscared.com/assessment. It takes about fifteen minutes to complete and will give you instant insight into your most dominant fear archetype.

While the Do It Scared Fear Assessment is a helpful tool for identifying the specific types of fears that may be keeping you stuck, there are a few essential points to keep in mind.

There are no "good" versus "bad" fear archetypes. Because the archetypes represent the way fear manifests itself in our lives, all seven archetypes do have negative-sounding names, but each archetype has both positive and negative qualities.

Your fear archetype can change, based on current life circumstances and particular seasons of life, but it is also greatly impacted by deeper factors, such as childhood experiences or trauma.

The higher your percentage score for a particular archetype, the more likely it is that the archetype is affecting your life. It is quite possible that your levels for all seven archetypes will be in the low to middle range, in which case fear may be less of an issue for you; similarly, it could be that you score high in several categories.

HOW TO USE THIS BOOK

This book is meant to be a practical tool—a guidebook—to help you face your fears, overcome adversity, and, most importantly, create a life you love. Equal parts inspiration, practical application, and tough love, it will challenge you to rethink some of the limiting beliefs that might have you stuck and motivate you to make the changes necessary to move forward.

Our journey together begins in part 1 by understanding the seven unique ways fear manifests in our lives, both by identifying and learning more about your own unique fear archetype and the ways fear may be holding you back and by understanding the way fear may be manifesting for others around you. Here you'll identify specific areas you may need to focus on so you can make faster progress. This section can be a lot of fun, as you will most likely recognize aspects of yourself and people you know in at least a few of our archetype personas. Just keep in mind that whatever your archetype, there are always at least a few action steps you must take in order to move forward, and those will be addressed here.

In part 2, we'll explore the Principles of Courage—seven core beliefs that, once adopted as your own, can radically transform your mind-set and give you the courage to make changes you previously may have believed were impossible.

And finally, in part 3, Courage in Action, we'll identify some practical tools you can use to put these changes into practice in concrete ways.

Do It Scared is designed to be a quick, fun read, but you'll definitely want to digest it slowly, and maybe even read some chapters more than once. Be sure to have a highlighter, pen, and notebook at the ready, because I guarantee you'll want to take some notes. And to take a deeper dive into overcoming the role of fear in your own life, be sure to take advantage of our additional resources and worksheets at doitscared.com, which are designed to help you apply all the lessons you're learning here in a real and practical way in your own life. Likewise, the *Do It Scared with Ruth Soukup* podcast is a great way to reinforce the messages you'll be learning here and to get weekly inspiration and encouragement.

Here's to facing your fears, overcoming adversity, and creating a life you love.

Here's to **doing it scared**.

PART ONE

the fear archetypes

When it comes to facing the obstacles that hold us back or keep us from pursuing our goals and dreams, not all fear is created equal, nor does it always manifest itself in the same way. The seven fear archetypes represent the unique ways fear can show up in our lives.

The good news is, once we identify the type of fear that is negatively impacting our life, holding us back, or keeping us stuck, we can actually do something about it.

Of course, confronting the biggest fears that are keeping you stuck starts by taking the Do It Scared Fear Assessment, which will give you instant insight into your psyche. So buckle up and discover your own fear archetype at doitscared.com/assessment.

chapter one

the procrastinator

When you're most afraid of making a mistake

Perfectionism is not as much the desire for excellence as it is the fear of failure couched in procrastination.	*Dan Miller, 48 Days to the Work You Love*

Alice has always liked things to be just so.

She's incredibly particular about the way she dresses, how she does her hair, and the way she decorates her home. It's important to her that these things be *right*, even if she can't always explain what "right" is. In fact, she'll sometimes spend hours tweaking the smallest things—changing her top or shoes or accessories, or moving a vase or photo frame around the room—just trying to get them right.

Preferring to get things right is a theme that comes up a lot for Alice. The truth is that the thought of making a mistake terrifies her, sometimes so much that she is afraid to begin at all. To compensate for this fear, she often starts working on a project early in order to give herself as much time as possible, because she knows she'll probably be tweaking right up until the last minute, wanting to make sure everything is just the way it should be.

As a student, she often tried to get ahead on her schoolwork, sometimes starting before the teacher had even handed out the assignment. Even so, she never turned in an assignment until the very last minute, sometimes even pulling all-nighters just to check and double-check everything one more time and to tweak it until it was perfect. But when there was an assignment she really dreaded, she'd put it off almost indefinitely.

These days, Alice works as a graphic designer for a fast-growing, start-up coffee company. She likes the work (and the coffee), but she also finds it very stressful. Because the company is growing so quickly, things are constantly changing, and it feels like almost every project she's asked to work on is needed ASAP, which doesn't give Alice any time to get ahead. Her boss has no idea that she often stays up half the night endlessly tweaking her designs in order to get them done on time. The lack of sleep, the constant change, and the intense pressure she puts on herself to make sure everything is always perfect are starting to wear Alice down.

Change makes Alice extremely uncomfortable. She prefers to stick to a routine and to the things she knows really well. Her friends and her husband sometimes tease her about being rigid, but Alice prefers to think of herself as being consistent. Even so, that need for consistency can hold her back sometimes. She feels anxious about saying yes to anything that is too far outside of her comfort zone, even when there's a part of her that would like to break free. When she was asked recently by her church to participate in a mission trip to Kenya, she was too afraid to commit. "It just feels so far away," she said, "and there are so many unknowns!"

Because her job is so stressful, Alice has thought a lot about branching out on her own and becoming a freelance graphic designer. The thought of being able to work from home and set her own hours is appealing, but she is also terrified of making a mistake or misstep when it comes to starting her own business. In fact, she is so afraid of failing that she just can't seem to take that step. Sometimes she feels paralyzed.

Alice has high expectations of herself and of everyone around her. When she and her husband fight, he accuses her of being a perfectionist. Alice doesn't understand why that's such a bad thing. What's wrong with wanting things to be perfect? In her mind, it's better to not do something at all than to do it and have it not be right.

Alice is a Procrastinator.

THE PROCRASTINATOR™ ARCHETYPE

Also known as the Perfectionist, the Procrastinator archetype struggles most with the fear of making a mistake, which often manifests itself as a fear of commitment, or a fear of getting started. Because she is terrified of making a wrong move, the Procrastinator looks for—and often finds—any number of perfectly legitimate reasons not to begin or not to try at all.

Ironically, on the surface, the Procrastinator often exhibits behavior that seems to be the *opposite* of procrastination, such as planning things far in advance or trying to work ahead. It's important to realize that for the Procrastinator, procrastination doesn't necessarily occur in the traditional sense of simply putting everything off until the last minute. Instead, the Procrastinator wants to avoid making any mistakes and will therefore try to give herself as much time as possible for a task.

As a general rule, when push comes to shove, the Procrastinator is afraid to act and can often find herself paralyzed by indecision, especially when decisive action must be taken quickly. The Procrastinator prefers to spend an inordinate amount of time researching, planning, or getting organized. While this high level of preparation can be advantageous, it can also stymie progress when the research, planning, and organization become a substitute for taking action.

At their core, Procrastinators are terrified of messing up or making a huge mistake, especially one that cannot be reversed, and this intense fear can prevent them from moving forward toward their goals and dreams. They often require an outside influence or deadline to compel them to act; left to their own devices, they will sometimes put things off indefinitely.

According to our survey, the Procrastinator is the most common of all the fear archetypes, with 41 percent of people showing this as their top archetype, and 74 percent having this archetype in their top three.

POSITIVE ATTRIBUTES

The Procrastinator's desire for perfection fuels a drive for high achievement. She values excellence and holds herself to a very high standard, which generally results in a high quality of work. The Procrastinator is very good at tasks that require a fanatical attention to detail or extreme diligence in preparation. Moreover, the Procrastinator's thoroughness in research and preparation results in fewer errors and a better end result.

Procrastinators prefer order and organization and tend to be good at creating systems. They are often focused, driven, and diligent, and they possess a strong work ethic. They are task and results oriented. The Procrastinator is often drawn to and excels at occupations that require a fanatical attention to detail, such as scientific research, engineering, writing and editing, interior design, graphic design, teaching, and administration.

HABITS AND BEHAVIORS

- Likes to plan ahead in order to allow as much time as possible
- Often plans vacations and major projects months or even years in advance
- Tends to be detail oriented
- Postpones or avoids things they don't feel competent in
- Is naturally drawn to order and organization
- Often checks and double-checks to make sure things are perfect

- Never feels like things are "ready"
- Loves research and feels like there is always more to learn about a topic
- Can be extremely self-critical
- Gets depressed or extremely upset at mistakes
- Is schedule oriented and acutely aware of deadlines

AT A GLANCE
The Procrastinator

- Is a perfectionist who likes things to be "right"
- Fears making a mistake and has trouble "pulling the trigger"
- Can spend too much time researching and planning
- Typically produces high-quality work
- Tends to be well organized
- Gives great attention to detail

THE VOICE OF THE PROCRASTINATOR

One of the most powerful parts of the survey was the comments people made to describe their fears. Each archetype has its own voice, its own unique way of expressing what fear looks and feels like. All the statements below are quotes from respondents who received a high Procrastinator score.

- "I feel so embarrassed about not achieving perfection that it prevents me from even getting started."
- "I'm always worried that I don't have all the correct information I need to move forward."
- "I hate the feeling of being uncomfortable in a situation that is unknown. I get nervous about change, and I'm always afraid of failure when it comes to doing new things."

- "I'm just afraid of failing. I don't know how I would handle failing at my 'big goal,' and that is what holds me back from starting. I don't want to let my husband and son down if I fail, and I don't want others to look at me for my failure and not see what I accomplish every day in my current work situation."
- "I'm afraid of failing and sometimes of achieving. Basically, I think I'm afraid of change, so my inner mind holds me back because what I know now is 'safe.'"
- "I am afraid that I will fail. I am also afraid to put myself out there in case I do fail. I find it really uncomfortable to be put in new situations."

HOW THIS FEAR ARCHETYPE CAN HOLD YOU BACK

While there is a lot to admire about the Procrastinator's attention to detail and almost fanatical commitment to excellence, the overriding fear of making a mistake or of committing to an irreversible course of action can hinder her willingness to take risks, try new things, or commit to big, scary goals.

Here are some ways that being a Procrastinator can adversely affect you and hold you back:

- You worry so much about planning far in advance that you neglect to take advantage of the immediate opportunities right in front of you.
- You say no too often.
- You feel paralyzed by the thought of making a mistake—so much so that it prevents you from taking even a first step.
- You never feel quite ready to begin, and so you don't.
- You spend so much time researching, planning, and organizing that you never actually get started.
- You have trouble committing to deadlines.

- You struggle to meet your own high expectations and rarely feel completely satisfied with your work.
- You have trouble finishing important projects because you feel like there is always more tweaking and perfecting that could be done.
- You struggle with giving yourself grace or giving yourself the freedom to try new things and make mistakes.
- You experience anxiety and fear when you don't have enough time for research and planning.

STRATEGIES TO OVERCOME THIS FEAR

If you're a Procrastinator, here are a few strategies you can use to overcome your fear of making a mistake.

Reframe

When you can start looking at life as a series of *lessons* rather than mistakes, it will give you more freedom to experiment rather than always striving to achieve perfection. For the Procrastinator, the fear of making a mistake or a misstep is so paralyzing that it can prevent them from taking any action at all. Of course, without taking action, you'll never be able to accomplish any of those big goals and dreams that percolate in your head, which is why it's so important to learn how to reframe the way you view mistakes or the way you look at all imperfections and things that go wrong.

Take Action

One simple but incredibly effective change you can make immediately is to start inserting more hard deadlines into your calendar—deadlines that have consequences when you don't meet them. It could be a self-inflicted penalty, or you could call in reinforcements from outside sources—perhaps ask your spouse or a trusted friend or even your boss to set the date and determine the penalty. Just keep in mind that the more "real" you can make the deadlines, the more likely you will be to stick to them.

As a Procrastinator, your natural tendency can often be to put as much time between you and the deadline as possible. Sometimes that means planning too far in advance; sometimes it means waiting until the last minute. Either way, it means that more than anything else, you need a finish line!

Make a point of practicing imperfect action—do one thing each day just to do it, not because it needs to be "right." For example, you might practice turning in a work assignment as a rough draft, rather than the final product, just to see how it feels. In the end, action is truly the only antidote to fear, which means that the more you practice taking action—even small steps in the right direction—the easier it will become to take larger steps and more dramatic action.

Create Accountability

An accountability partner is someone who supports, encourages, and challenges you to keep a commitment. (We'll talk more about how to work with an accountability partner in chapters 11 and 18.) The key thing for a Procrastinator is to find an accountability partner who is *not* a fellow Procrastinator. Only someone who has different strengths and a different fear archetype than you do can provide the alternative perspective you need. Look for someone who encourages you to take action and to keep moving forward, even when things aren't quite perfect, and who will call you out when you put things off or feel afraid to commit.

MOVING PAST PERFECTION

Alice knows she will probably always be a person who likes things "just so," but she has also actively begun to take steps to overcome the fears about failing and making mistakes that have kept her stuck.

She started by posting a sign on her desk that read, "There are no mistakes, only lessons." She's not sure she actually believes it just yet, but she likes having the reminder front and center. And over the past couple of weeks, she has noticed that the anxiety and panic she has always felt just before turning in a new project have actually diminished significantly.

Alice has also begun to set a timer for completing certain tasks, in addition to giving herself firm deadlines for each large project. This has helped her stop the endless tweaking, and she's realizing that her work might even be better as a result. Her boss hasn't seemed to notice any change in quality, but Alice feels a lot less stressed by all the changes being thrown her way.

While she is starting to enjoy her job a lot more, Alice's new-found freedom to make mistakes has prompted her to think more seriously about branching out on her own as a freelancer. To give herself encouragement and support, Alice joined a Facebook group of independent graphic designers. She's been able to make some great connections and get answers to many of her questions about freelance life. When a few of the designers encouraged her to ask her boss if he would consider hiring her as a part-time contractor while she established her freelance business, she took action and followed through. Lo and behold, her boss said yes!

Alice never realized just how much her need for perfection was impacting her life, but now she sees just how much her fear of making mistakes had been holding her back in so many different areas. What's more, she is amazed at how much happier and fulfilled she feels now that she is actively working to push past that fear—even if it sometimes means making a mistake.

do it scared

Need more tips for dealing with procrastination and perfectionism? Pay close attention to the lessons in chapters 8, 12, 17, and 21.

chapter two

the rule follower

When you're most afraid of coloring outside the lines

> Learn the rules like a pro so you can break them like an artist.
>
> *Sometimes attributed to Pablo Picasso*

Tracy has always played it straight.

As a kid, she was responsible and dependable, the one who never stepped out of line or questioned her teachers. She worked hard. She colored inside the lines. She followed all the rules—to the letter. And from a very early age, she knew she wanted a career in law enforcement.

After four years in the military, Tracy became a police officer in a city just twenty miles from where she grew up. For the most part, she loved her job. The law was clear and unambiguous, and she genuinely liked knowing exactly what was expected of her. She put in her time, played by the rules, and moved up the ranks, just like she was supposed to.

In her free time, Tracy volunteered in the community and was an active member of her church. She and her husband bought a few acres outside of town, and after her three children were born, they began growing their own vegetables as a family project. Gardening soon became an obsession for Tracy; she loved seeing how the more effort she put in—and the more careful she was about providing just the right amount of water and fertilizer—the better results she got.

She loved canning and pickling and was soon giving away her homemade salsas and spicy pickles as gifts to her friends and family. They couldn't get enough.

For Tracy, life was steady and predictable, just the way she liked it.

And then she got hurt.

Unfortunately for Tracy, her injury didn't happen at work, which would have guaranteed an early retirement and disability benefits. Instead, it was just a silly thing, really. While helping a friend move, she slipped on a step and tore a ligament and some cartilage in her knee.

She was removed from the field and assigned to temporary desk duty, but that assignment ultimately became permanent when her knee failed to heal correctly. The reassignment meant a demotion and a significant pay cut.

And for Tracy, life suddenly didn't feel quite as steady or predictable as before.

With three years to go before she could begin collecting her pension, Tracy knew she had to find some way to supplement her income, so she began selling her homemade relishes and salsa at the local farmers market. Tracy was great at researching interesting flavor combinations and incorporating them into her products. They were delicious and incredibly popular, and she began to amass a local following.

Now a few of her most loyal customers are encouraging her to go bigger with this fledgling business—to create a brand for her products and maybe even start selling online. However, while Tracy is eager to earn more money, she's also hesitant to move forward. She knows there are a ton of regulations related to selling food, and she just doesn't know how she could ever meet all the requirements. Selling at a farmers market is one thing—the laws are pretty relaxed—but actually creating a real business and selling online and perhaps even shipping out of state seems completely out of her league. Where can she even begin to find a list of all the requirements? And what if she misses something? The thought of violating a major regulation or getting into trouble terrifies her. Every time she even ponders the idea, she feels paralyzed.

There is just no way. And now she feels stuck.

Tracy is a Rule Follower.

THE RULE FOLLOWER™ ARCHETYPE

Often sticklers for doing things the way they are "supposed" to be done, those who exemplify the Rule Follower archetype struggle most with an outsized fear of authority, a fear that often manifests itself as an irrational aversion to breaking the rules or doing anything that may be perceived as "not allowed." Just the possibility of getting in trouble—even when the potential "punishment" is only imagined—is enough to prevent the Rule Follower from taking action or moving forward.

Rule Followers see the world in black and white and tend to feel anxious anytime they sense themselves or other people stepping outside the norms of acceptable behavior. They can be preoccupied with making sure other people are making good decisions and can sometimes be perceived as nosy.

At her core, the Rule Follower believes that if things are not done according to the rules, chaos will ensue. Her mind-set is that many things in life just are the way they are, and they shouldn't be questioned or changed. The Rule Follower feels energized when she is proven right or when a decision she has made is shown to be correct.

Rule Followers often forgo their own best judgment in favor of following the rules because their irrational fear of stepping outside the lines overrides everything else. This fear can also prevent Rule Followers from taking action toward their own goals or dreams. They are often afraid to trust their gut or to take an action that does not feel clear and straightforward.

Rule Followers tend to be conformist and can also be somewhat rigid. They like to know that there is a "right" way to do things, and they take comfort in following the established norms. They are uncomfortable with the idea of thinking outside the box or forging their own path, and they can sometimes be judgmental toward people who don't toe the line like they do.

The Rule Follower is the second most common fear archetype, with 14 percent of people showing this as their top archetype, and 64 percent having this archetype in their top three.

POSITIVE ATTRIBUTES

The Rule Follower is responsible, trustworthy, and a very loyal friend and employee. She tends to be exceptionally diligent, thorough, and stable, as well as thoughtful and considerate, and she can be counted on to look out for other people.

The Rule Follower has a clear sense of right and wrong, excellent discernment, and a strong moral code. This sense of duty and obligation to others and to the community at large is often seen in a commitment to volunteer work or public service.

The Rule Follower also tends to be meticulous about details and is exceptionally good at follow-through, always taking care to dot the i's and cross the t's. She takes the time to read the fine print and to make sure she has done her due diligence. Because they like knowing that there is a right and a wrong way of doing things, Rule Followers are often naturally drawn to careers that have very clear guidelines and a well-established, straightforward path to follow, such as law enforcement, engineering, mathematics, computer programming, public service, law, and medicine.

- Often has an outsized fear of authority
- Is nervous about breaking the rules or not doing something the way it's "supposed" to be done
- May adhere to a rule or the status quo at the expense of her own judgment
+ Tends to be extremely trustworthy and responsible
+ Is loyal, thoughtful, and considerate
+ Possesses a strong sense of duty and of right and wrong

HABITS AND BEHAVIORS

- Prefers for things to be done the "right" way, in the "right" order
- Likes knowing there is an established plan or protocol to follow
- Looks out for others to make sure they are making good decisions
- Tends to see the world in black and white
- Is reluctant to step outside the lines; worries about getting "in trouble"
- Is frequently a creature of habit; likes order and routine
- Works hard to maintain stability and predictability in her life
- Likes to be right
- Avoids chaos and uncertainty

THE VOICE OF THE RULE FOLLOWER

In our fear study, these were some of the thoughts and beliefs expressed by respondents who received a high Rule Follower score.

- "I'm most worried about the unknown and uncharted territory where I may not have a support system to show me the way."
- "I like it when someone shows me exactly what to do or gives me a plan to follow. I will follow the plan to the letter, as long as I know it works!"
- "It makes me upset when others don't follow the rules or do things the right way."
- "I always have to make sure that I know everything I need to know and that I'm in compliance with any regulations governing what I do."
- "I have spent my adult life seeking permission. I'm always worried that what I want to do might not be allowed."
- "I struggle with knowing exactly what to do and doing it the 'right' way without mistakes."
- "I really don't like the idea of getting it wrong."
- "I am most scared about whether or not I'm making the 'right' decision. I often think that if I make the decision to go with this option, then what am I missing out on by not choosing the other option?"

HOW THIS FEAR ARCHETYPE CAN HOLD YOU BACK

While the Rule Follower does have a lot of positive and admirable qualities, the irrational fear of breaking the rules, doing something the wrong way, or potentially getting in trouble can be a huge hindrance when it comes to trying new things or setting and achieving big goals. In fact, the Rule Follower will often rule out an option before even giving it a chance, just because it feels like doing it the "right" way would be impossible.

Here are some ways that being a Rule Follower can adversely affect you and hold you back:

- While you might sometimes dream of doing something new, you will often avoid taking risks, such as switching careers, starting a business, moving to a new city, or going back to school.
- You may be susceptible to peer pressure or to going along with a popular idea, simply because it's the status quo and not necessarily because it serves you.
- You may struggle with giving yourself grace or embracing the freedom to try new things and make mistakes.
- You may have difficulty maintaining a positive relationship with nonconformists or people who have shown poor judgment in some area of their lives. Your tendency to see things in black and white can cause you to be rigid and unforgiving.
- Your unhealthy fear of authority may cause you to acquiesce to the demands of someone in a position of power rather than take a stand or use your own judgment.
- You may experience anxiety and fear when you don't have a specific path or plan of action.
- You may let set beliefs about your own gender, race, religion, social status, or educational level dictate what you believe you are capable of.

STRATEGIES TO OVERCOME THIS FEAR

Here are a few strategies to help you move past your fear of doing something that's not allowed.

Reframe

It's not always easy to write your own rules, especially when you are most comfortable with following *other* people's rules. Even so, taking the time to create and adopt your own set of principles—the basic core values you want to follow in your own life—can help alleviate the constant pressure you feel from adhering to everyone else's norms. Your principles don't need to be elaborate or even completely original, but they should ring true to you and fit within your own set of core beliefs. These will give you your own set of guidelines to follow—a set of guidelines that should overrule the "rules" you hear from other people and outside sources.

Approach this set of principles both proactively and reactively. First, proactively write a rough draft of your principles to remind yourself of the way you prefer to live your life. Second, take a specific situation that challenges you and identify the spoken or unspoken rule you feel compelled to abide by. Third, rewrite the rule so it affirms your own principles and rules to live by. For example, an unwritten (and unachievable!) "rule" in many organizations is, "Give it your all, or you will not succeed and you will feel guilty." Rewrite that rule to be, "I will give X—and no more. And I will not allow anyone to make me feel guilty for giving X. I can be a success on my own terms."

Take Action

List the rules you are afraid of breaking and tackle them one by one. For a Rule Follower, the urge to comply with the way things are supposed to be can be overwhelming. When you take the time to write out those rules, you'll realize they aren't really "rules" at all, or that the rules can easily be researched and complied with. Not all rules are bad, but fear of breaking the rules shouldn't be what holds you back. Rewrite the narrative in your head, and you just may discover that the rules you were so afraid of breaking aren't actually as important as you thought they were.

And while you're at it, practice "breaking the rules" and stepping outside of your comfort zone in ways that don't feel overly risky. This can be something like daring to speak up when someone is being rude, rearranging your furniture in new and creative ways, or maybe even skipping the directions if you've never done that before, just for the sake of pushing your limits. Start with the small things, and you may be amazed at how much easier the big things become! As a Rule Follower, your comfort zone tends to be very well-defined. Therefore, if you want to become more comfortable with doing hard things, taking risks, and daring to take action in the face of fear, it will be helpful to start small.

Create Accountability

As a Rule Follower, you will need to find an accountability partner who is *not* a Rule Follower. Instead, look for someone who has different strengths, a different outlook, or a different fear archetype than you do and will provide an alternative perspective on the rules you feel compelled to follow. Try to find someone who encourages you to use your own judgment and critical thinking skills rather than defaulting to the way things are "supposed to be"—someone who will hold you accountable when you might be looking at a situation in black-and-white terms.

MOVING PAST THE FEAR OF BREAKING THE RULES

One Saturday morning at the farmers market, one of Tracy's best customers, Jane, again commented that she wished Tracy would take her business to the next level and start selling online.

"Tracy, your flavors are incredible! The world needs your salsa!"

As always, Tracy smiled, sighed, and said wistfully, "I just don't know how I'd get past all those rules and regulations. I'm so afraid of doing something wrong that I don't know how I'd even begin."

But this time, Jane's response surprised her. "Well, why don't you go take a class or get some help with the regulations? I'm sure there must be some sort of conference or training for this sort of thing. You should look into it!"

Tracy was stunned. Why had she never thought of that?

The minute she got home from the market, she began doing

some research and discovered an e-commerce conference was happening the following month in a city just three hours away. She immediately registered for the conference and crossed her fingers that she was doing the right thing.

As it turned out, it was the best decision Tracy ever made.

At the conference, she signed up for the food-sellers track, where she took a class on how to navigate food safety rules and regulations. She got all her biggest questions answered, and she walked away with a clear plan of action for what to do next. But that wasn't all. She also made some great connections with other retailers who had already been selling online for a while and learned a ton about other aspects of e-commerce that had long intimidated her—things like how to build a website and how to handle sales and marketing. And while she was there, she signed up for an online coaching group that would provide support and instruction along the way.

Equipped with a set of "instructions" to follow, Tracy felt emboldened to move forward with her dream. She followed to the letter every step of the plan that had been laid out for her, and within a few months, she had set up her website and started selling online.

For the first time she can remember, Tracy feels excited about the unknown rather than scared of it. Facing her fears head-on has given her more confidence, and she can't wait to see what the future brings.

Need more tips for overcoming your fear of authority so you can dare to step outside the lines? Be sure to read chapters 9, 12, and 19.

chapter three

the people pleaser

When you're most afraid of what other people will think

You probably wouldn't worry about what people think of you if you could know how seldom they do.	*Olin Miller*

Everyone loves Mandy.

She's just so . . . *nice.* Thoughtful, kind, generous, and always willing to pitch in. In fact, she rarely says no because she hates disappointing anyone or letting people down.

Unfortunately it's a trait that sometimes makes her easy to take advantage of. Whether she's at work or church or even the PTA, everyone knows Mandy is the best person to ask when they need help or a favor, because she will always go above and beyond the call of duty. Sometimes her friends wonder how Mandy even finds time to sleep.

Mandy works as an office manager for a large construction company, and her boss adores her. And why wouldn't he? She is the model employee, coming in early and staying late, always making sure she has done the best possible job, sometimes even covering for coworkers who haven't quite measured up.

Mandy hates conflict and tension, so she spends a lot of time trying to smooth things over and make sure no one is upset or angry. Sometimes her boss teases her and calls her Pollyanna, because she's always trying to look on the bright side.

Mandy has been this way ever since she was a little girl. She grew up in a relatively happy family. They were almost picture-perfect—a mom and a dad with two kids, a girl and a boy, living in the suburbs in a comfortable split-level ranch home. But then Mandy's older brother started to rebel when he got into middle school, and by high school he always seemed to be in trouble. The fights at home were epic, and Mandy spent most of her time trying to be the perfect daughter and to keep the tension from bubbling over.

Mandy cares a lot about how she looks and what she wears because she's always concerned about what other people might think. She likes to keep up with the trends but doesn't like to be too cutting edge. She also takes a lot of pride in decorating and taking care of her home—she would never want anyone to think she wasn't a good homemaker!

Mandy has always had a busy social life and a lot of friends. She's fun to be around and genuinely lights up a room with her smile. Most of the time, Mandy and her husband get along great, mostly because Mandy hates to argue and will usually just go along with what he wants rather than fight for her own way.

Every once in a while, Mandy dreams about starting her own business—she would love to open a little coffee shop downtown—but she has no idea where she would find the time. And besides, she doesn't think she could bear the thought of what people would say, especially if the business failed. She would be mortified.

At times, Mandy finds her life exhausting. She spends so much time trying to make everyone else happy that there isn't a whole lot of time left to focus on her own hopes and dreams. Honestly, she's not even sure she knows what she wants.

Mandy is a People Pleaser.

THE PEOPLE PLEASER™ ARCHETYPE

Naturally drawn to seek the approval of others, the People Pleaser archetype struggles most with the fear of being judged, which also manifests itself as the fear of letting people down and the fear of what other people might say. Essentially, the People Pleaser's biggest concern can often be summed up as the fear of how others may react.

Because the People Pleaser is so afraid of being judged—or, worse yet, mocked or ridiculed—and because the People Pleaser is acutely aware of and fearful of how others might react or what they might say, she can sometimes be hesitant to move forward, find herself crippled with indecision, and feel unable to take action. Above all, she doesn't like the thought of making a fool of herself.

While they might not consider themselves extroverts, People Pleasers are often popular and well-liked. Because they are hyper-aware of how they might be perceived, they tend to choose their words carefully or sometimes even hide their true feelings about a subject if it seems to go against the general consensus.

That said, the People Pleaser can often be gregarious, funny, and engaging—the life of the party—which is a way of winning approval from others and being liked. She may also put a great deal of effort into her appearance, as well as be concerned with status symbols, such as a nice car, a well-appointed home, and designer labels.

The People Pleaser can sometimes get into the habit of being a "yes woman"—a person who always agrees and who may even shift her own viewpoints to go along with someone else. She likes to get along and is reluctant to do anything that might cause anger, disappointment, or hurt feelings.

People Pleasers can be overly interested in what other people think, which makes them susceptible to peer pressure. They have a deep desire to fit in and be part of the crowd.

While not necessarily coming across as meek, the People Pleaser has a hard time saying no, setting limits, and establishing healthy boundaries, because she is so afraid of letting other people down. Others tend to see her as being "a giver" or someone who is helpful and kind and generous with her time and energy.

While these characteristics can be a good thing, they can also lead People Pleasers to become overcommitted or to allow other people's priorities and requests to override their own goals and dreams. This can result in deep feelings of resentment or bitterness that will sometimes bubble to the surface in unexpected ways.

The People Pleaser is the third most common fear archetype, with 21 percent of people showing this as their top archetype, and 63 percent having this archetype in their top three.

POSITIVE ATTRIBUTES

People Pleasers are usually among the nicest, most thoughtful, and most generous people around. They are caring and considerate and go out of their way to help. They tend to be popular and well-liked and are often funny, friendly, and engaging.

This makes People Pleasers wonderful people to have as friends. They are great allies and fantastic employees who are reliable, professional, and well-spoken. People Pleasers can fit into almost any career path but are especially good in support roles or professions that allow them to work with people. Common occupations include administration, nursing, teaching, social work, customer service, and retail.

HABITS AND BEHAVIORS

- Is overly concerned about looking foolish, stupid, or silly
- Does not ever want to let people down
- Spends an inordinate amount of time worrying about what other people may think or say

- Tends to be popular and well-liked
- Can be overly concerned with outward appearance and status symbols; likes to "dress to impress"
- Dislikes going against popular opinion or general consensus; hides or changes personal views to fit in
- Fears losing friendships or being judged; avoids anything that may put a friendship at risk
- Says yes too often and can become overcommitted as a result
- Cares deeply about what other people think
- Is often seen as funny, warm, generous, and kind
- Has a deep desire to fit in and be part of the crowd

AT A GLANCE
The People Pleaser

- ⊖ Derives self-worth from the approval of others
- ⊖ Has trouble saying no and struggles to set boundaries
- ⊖ Hesitates to take action and fears what others think
- ⊕ Is typically well-liked and fun to be around
- ⊕ Is thoughtful, considerate, and generous
- ⊕ Is a responsible employee and great team player

THE VOICE OF THE PEOPLE PLEASER

Here are some of the thoughts and beliefs expressed by our fear study respondents who received a high People Pleaser score.

- "I'm afraid of failure and of being ridiculed or being laughed at. I'm worried about losing my friends."

- "I know I shouldn't be, but I'm afraid of what others think about me and what I am doing. I'm worried that they won't approve."
- "I'm afraid of looking stupid, of having people think I'm wasting money, and of disappointing those I love or making them angry in some way."
- "I'm scared of getting overwhelmed and then letting people down. I love to try to learn new things, but when someone else is depending on it, I get nervous. I've let people down before due to lack of time, lack of stamina, or lack of willpower, and that makes me wary of my limits. That's the reason I often undershoot or reject opportunities."
- "I'm always nervous about what others will say and how they will respond."
- "I booked a couple of workshops to speak about health and focusing on self-love and overcoming emotional eating, and then I canceled the talks—all of them. I let my fear of being seen and judged as not qualified stop me."
- "I'm scared of falling flat on my face in front of other people or seeming like a faker. I'm worried about standing out among my peers and being worse than my peers who have become 'pros.'"
- "I'm worried about making mistakes and disappointing people. I don't want to embarrass myself."

HOW THIS FEAR ARCHETYPE CAN HOLD YOU BACK

As a People Pleaser, you face the danger of allowing the thoughts, opinions, and needs of others to prevent you from pursuing your own dreams, passions, and goals.

Here are some ways that being a People Pleaser can adversely affect you and hold you back:

- You may avoid taking action or pursuing a goal because you're worried and fearful about what others may think or say.
- You may be susceptible to peer pressure or to going along with a popular idea or viewpoint simply because it's what everyone else seems to be doing and because you want to fit in.
- You may struggle with saying no to requests, which leaves you overcommitted and with little time for pursuing your own goals and dreams.
- You may have a tendency to let people take advantage of your kindness and generosity or to "walk all over you."
- Your irrational fear of letting people down may cause you to give in to the demands of others rather than take a stand or use your own judgment.
- You may experience anxiety and fear when you feel like you are being judged or have the potential to be judged in some way.
- You may be more concerned with being liked and getting others' approval than pursuing your own goals and dreams.

STRATEGIES TO OVERCOME THIS FEAR

Here are a few strategies you can use to overcome your fear of being judged or of letting people down.

Reframe

A big part of your fear of being judged or of letting people down comes from the script that plays inside your head—a script that says others might not love or accept you if you don't perform the way you think they want you to. If you want to break free of this fear, you need to start modifying that voice in your head. Create some new affirmations you can repeat to yourself daily that change the message that is being played.

If deep down you believe that others may judge you or not like you for saying no, then perhaps your new affirmation could be something like, "It's okay to have my own opinion and for other people to disagree. Disagreement doesn't mean they don't like me." Likewise, if your fear is that people will be disappointed in you, try telling yourself something like, "The people who matter are not disappointed when I set boundaries." Sometimes it is just a matter of making small changes to the script that is already playing.

Take Action

For the People Pleaser, the most important thing to practice is saying the word *no*! After all, if you refuse to say no, it won't be long until you get to a point where you're unable to give 100 percent to anyone or anything. Worse yet, you'll begin to resent the tasks you've taken on, as well as the rest of the things in your life that you really *should* be doing and *could* be doing if you had just said no. Over-commitment is a downward spiral that is best avoided by saying no. Of course, for a People Pleaser, this is easier said than done! But like anything else in life, the more you practice, the better you become. So do whatever it takes to get proficient, whether it's asking for time to decide, delegating the task to someone else, or having someone say no on your behalf. But do say no. Again and again and again.

At the same time, give yourself permission to practice self-care and to make time for your own dreams, goals, and priorities. Block out time in your schedule that is just for you. You may have to start small at first, and it may take some time for other people to adjust, but know that when you are caring for your own needs, you are making yourself better for others as well.

As a People Pleaser, you've likely been putting other people's needs before your own for quite some time, and neglecting your own self-care may be wearing you down. But just as it is with air masks on an airplane—where the protocol is to put on your own mask before assisting others—it's important to take care of yourself so you can be there for others.

Create Accountability

One of the best things you can do to overcome any type of fear is to find a teacher or mentor who embodies the qualities and skills you're hoping to develop and allow her to guide you. If you can, find someone with a different fear archetype—perhaps an Outcast—to help balance out your people-pleasing tendencies.

Ideally, you'll find someone who is willing to push you beyond your comfort zone—someone who will also help you practice saying no and take care of yourself. It may feel uncomfortable at first, but eventually, especially with the help of someone you admire and trust, you can get there.

MOVING PAST THE NEED TO PLEASE

Mandy was practically on the verge of a nervous breakdown, and yet she was afraid to let anyone know, for fear that she would let them down. She knew something had to give. As she tried to keep up with all her commitments, she was exhausted from doing too much and not getting enough sleep.

Then a rough bout with the flu put her over the edge. Unable to get out of bed, she listened to a podcast about self-care and saying no, and she finally recognized it was time to make some changes.

Mandy started by having a heart-to-heart with her husband, who was glad to hear that she was going to start making more time for herself. He told her he would love her no matter what, even if she didn't always go along with what he wanted to do.

For Mandy, that was huge.

She then started saying no—gracefully bowing out of a few commitments she had previously said yes to. She was flabbergasted when everyone she spoke to seemed to understand, and not a single person was angry. She realized that the pressure she was putting on herself may have been mostly in her head.

At work, she stopped trying to fix every conflict, and instead she began to encourage team members to work things out among themselves. She also started to be more careful about setting boundaries when it came to her schedule.

But the biggest change for Mandy has been the mind-set shift and the fact that she has given herself permission to make her own needs a priority. She still hasn't quite worked up the courage to start her coffee shop, but she's getting closer every day.

Need more tips for moving past the fear of being judged and letting people down, and the tendency to put other people's needs above your own? Be sure to read chapters 8, 13, and 19!

chapter four

the outcast

When you're most afraid of rejection

I am good at walking away. Rejection teaches you how to reject.	*Jeanette Winterson, Weight*

Vivian is not exactly the type of person *anyone* would describe as "fearful."

In fact, most of the time she appears to be just the opposite—completely fearless, a person who writes her own rules and lives life on her own terms. She's outspoken, confident, and bold. She marches to the beat of her own drum and doesn't seem to care what anyone else thinks. She's always up for adventure, loves to travel, and can hardly stay in one place.

She works in the tech industry as an independent contractor—a job that gives her plenty of freedom and independence and allows her to move around a lot for short-term projects. That's just the way she likes it, because every time Vivian has tried to work for someone else for any longer than a year or so, it hasn't gone all that well.

The companies she has worked for are always impressed by her ability to get in there and get the job done, even if she sometimes ruffles a few feathers along the way. Vivian is never afraid to speak up or say the controversial things others don't dare say out loud, but sometimes her blunt communication style can get her into trouble.

The truth is that Vivian tends to be pretty skeptical of most people, and if pressed, she'll admit she may have some trust issues. And while she can be a lot of fun, there are only a handful of people in her life she would consider part of her inner circle—people she trusts enough to consider them true friends.

Even so, she is always hurt when she feels like she is being left out or excluded—when her coworkers go out for drinks after work or make plans for the weekend and she's not invited. She pretends she doesn't care, but she does.

Growing up, Vivian was the middle of three girls, and she always felt like the black sheep of her family. Her two sisters were both athletic and popular, adored by everyone, including her parents, while Vivian always felt like the one who didn't belong. She was more interested in the "geeky" stuff, as her sisters called it— drama club, computers, and art—activities the rest of her family just couldn't seem to understand or appreciate.

And while she knew on some level that her family did care about her, she never really felt fully loved or accepted by them. It seemed like they were too busy going to every soccer, volleyball, and basketball game to bother with art shows or robotics competitions. Vivian always tried to act like she didn't care, but deep down, it really hurt.

In high school, she started to embrace her black-sheep reputation. She figured if people were going to consider her the rebel of the family, she may as well live up to her reputation. She pushed a lot of boundaries and questioned a lot of rules, and she always seemed to be in trouble for one thing or another.

After high school she decided to travel for a year before going to college, and even now, all these years later, she knows it's one of the best decisions she ever made—for the first time in her life, she wasn't living in her sisters' shadows.

These days, Vivian gets along with her sisters okay, now that they're older and have families of their own. With a respectable job and an impressive income, Vivian is no longer considered a troublemaker, but a big part of her still feels like she never quite fits in, and so she tends to keep her sisters at arm's length.

Vivian is an Outcast.

THE OUTCAST™ ARCHETYPE

The quintessential rugged individualist, the Outcast archetype struggles most with the fear of rejection, or a fear of trusting other people—a fear that often manifests itself by rejecting others before she has a chance to be rejected.

Ironically, to outside observers, the Outcast often appears to be fearless, a person who doesn't care what others think and who isn't at all afraid to forge her own path, to speak her mind, and to think outside the box and do things differently.

Inwardly, though, Outcasts often harbor a core belief that other people can't be counted on or trusted, and they tend to view even the mildest slight or dismissal as confirmation of that belief, which in turn causes them to reject others even more frequently. Even in situations where it is not personal and they're not *actually* being rejected, Outcasts will assume the worst.

Because they view themselves as unworthy of love and acceptance, Outcasts are often desperate to "prove" themselves to the world, whether it's through notable accomplishments, financial success, social status, or extreme behavior.

The Outcast tends to be a nonconformist, someone who rejects rules and limitations in favor of doing her own thing. She eschews conventionality and instead prefers to figure things out on her own. Again, from the outside, this makes the Outcast appear to be somewhat fearless, when in fact this "I don't care" attitude is a way of rejecting others before she can be rejected herself.

When taken to the extreme, the Outcast persona can sometimes result in self-destructive or criminal behavior. Because Outcasts tend to see the world as conspiring against them, they feel very little obligation to "color inside the lines." As a result, Outcasts can also be selfish and narcissistic, seeing life from only their own point of view, and they sometimes struggle to show empathy.

Outcasts have a difficult time working with a team, asking for help or assistance from others, or collaborating on group projects. They can sometimes lack tact, and they want to do things their way, without interference from others. They prefer to work independently.

Outcasts tend to have strong beliefs and opinions and are not generally afraid to share those opinions; on the contrary, Outcasts will sometimes use polarizing or controversial statements as a way of pushing other people away or rejecting them before they can be rejected.

The Outcast is the fourth most common fear archetype, with 15 percent of people showing this as their top archetype, and 38 percent having this archetype in their top three.

POSITIVE ATTRIBUTES

Outcasts tend to be driven, self-motivated, and determined to succeed (even if it's only to prove themselves), which means that Outcasts are often very successful. Their persistence keeps them going, even when many other people would quit, and they are also willing to take more risks than most people.

While not always a great team player, the Outcast can be a surprisingly good leader, when not derailed by trust issues or by polarizing statements. The Outcast is generally not afraid of making mistakes and is good at seizing opportunities, as well as taking ownership and responsibility.

As an individualist, the Outcast tends to be a good critical thinker and is capable of forming complex opinions. Outcasts tend to be drawn to career paths that allow for individual achievement and recognition and also allow them to think outside the box. They prefer to lead, not follow, and to do things completely on their own, which often draws them to careers in entrepreneurship, business, acting, directing, writing, art, or independent contractorship.

AT A GLANCE
The Outcast

- Fears rejection; will often push people away in order to avoid being rejected first
- Appears to be fearless and unfazed by what others think
- Sometimes struggles as part of a team; may self-destruct
- Is self-motivated and driven to succeed
- Can be a very effective leader
- Is persistent and willing to take risks; not easily discouraged by failure

HABITS AND BEHAVIORS

- Tends to believe that people will ultimately always let you down
- Is often afraid to let people get too close
- Tends to have just a few very close relationships
- Prefers to "go deep" in conversation rather than engage in pleasantries
- Is generally unafraid to speak her mind or tell people what she thinks; can sometimes be seen as a jerk or a blowhard as a result
- Often feels like she doesn't fit in or belong

- Can be sensitive to any perceived rejection, real or not, and is often overly or unreasonably offended by someone canceling plans or not including her
- Sometimes lacks tact or empathy
- Can be selfish and narcissistic; wants things the way she wants them
- Sometimes has difficulty with collaboration and teamwork
- Isn't afraid to take risks, try new things, or think outside the box
- Dislikes going along with the crowd

THE VOICE OF THE OUTCAST

Here are some of the thoughts and beliefs expressed by survey respondents who received a high Outcast score.

- "I worry I won't be good enough for my business to succeed and that no one will buy my photography."
- "I hated having to work for other people—that's why I started my own business."
- "I went to a new place to meet new people. At first I was okay, but then I got really uneasy and anxious and worried that people wouldn't like me. I left the party. I was kicking myself afterward because I had planned to go, arranged to go, and went, but my fear of being disliked got the better of me."
- "I don't want to put myself out there only to have the door slammed in my face."
- "I feel like I'll never be accepted or recognized for what I've accomplished."
- "I'm terrified of becoming close with other people. I may make new friends, but because of my past, I'm too timid to face my fear and take a leap of faith to trust others."

- "I've learned that I can't rely on anyone, and if I want to get something done, I have to do it myself."
- "I feel like in the end, people will always let you down if you are counting on them too much."
- "My husband died a year ago, and I recently wanted to try online dating but then chickened out. I'm only forty and don't want to be alone forever, but I'm terrified to put myself out there for fear of rejection. I'm disappointed in myself but not enough to do something about it because I can rationalize it away."
- "I don't need to be part of the crowd. I like to do my own thing."

HOW THIS FEAR ARCHETYPE CAN HOLD YOU BACK

While Outcasts often appear to be fearless—speaking their mind, trying new things, choosing to be independent, and daring to take risks—their fear of rejection can frequently hold them back in ways that aren't always immediately apparent.

Here are some ways that being an Outcast can adversely affect you and hold you back:

- You may harbor a core belief that people cannot be trusted, which makes you reluctant to open up or make yourself vulnerable. This can prevent you from fostering deep and meaningful relationships or even from cultivating useful business connections.
- You may be extremely sensitive to any perceived rejection, even if you aren't actually being rejected.
- You can be so driven to prove yourself through achievement that your success comes at the expense of other people and relationships.

- You often have trouble working with and collaborating with others.
- You may take risks or make decisions that are dangerous, potentially unhealthy, or illegal.
- You may push away people who are trying to help you.
- You may experience anxiety and fear when you feel like you're being left out.
- You can sometimes lack empathy or a filter. This may in turn be perceived negatively by others, which only adds to your feelings of being rejected.
- You can be stubborn and selfish and too often want things to be exactly your way.
- You are introverted or antisocial and simply don't enjoy the company of most people.

STRATEGIES TO OVERCOME THIS FEAR

If you are an Outcast, here are a few strategies you can use to overcome your fear of rejection.

Reframe

As with most of the other archetypes, a big part of your fear comes from the script that plays inside your head—in this case, the beliefs that people cannot be trusted and that it's better to reject others before they reject you.

If you want to push past this fear, you must reframe this message, create a new script, and develop different affirmations you can repeat to yourself daily that change the message that is being played.

For example, if deep down you believe that people can't be trusted, begin telling yourself things such as, "Just because people have hurt me in the past doesn't mean all people are untrustworthy. There are many people in my life who can be trusted." Likewise, if your fear is that people will reject you or let you down, perhaps you can rewrite that script to say, "Just because someone tells me no or disagrees with my idea doesn't mean they are rejecting me as a person."

Take Action

In addition to rewriting the script that is currently playing in your head, you'll also need to take some steps to practice trusting and collaborating with others in real-life situations. This will help you confirm and validate these new beliefs.

Begin to actively look for ways to put yourself out there a little bit more, especially in situations you might normally shy away from. Perhaps ask for help when you would normally do it yourself or join a group when your natural instinct is to go it alone. If your trust issues run deep, consider going to a counselor to explore what may lie at the heart of your fear.

Most importantly, try to put your "rejection" guard down, and don't assume you're being rejected anytime someone says no. Most of the time, they are not rejecting you!

Create Accountability

As an Outcast, you struggle with allowing yourself to become vulnerable. It's important, then, to actively work on opening yourself up, even if only to one or two trusted accountability partners. This will most likely feel completely unnatural at first. Even so, seeking out accountability and honest feedback is crucial to overcoming fear. Your accountability partner will help you spot those times your inner Outcast is putting up your defenses and will be able to help you move past your fear of being rejected.

You may also want to consider opening yourself up to some sort of mentor and allowing him or her to guide you. As an Outcast, you may find this to be particularly difficult, since you're not accustomed to seeking out the help of others, but doing so will push you outside of your comfort zone in precisely the way you need to be pushed. It won't feel natural at first to work with a mentor, but eventually, especially with the help of someone you admire and trust, you will experience the benefit of working with another person in a collaborative way.

MOVING PAST REJECTION

The first hint that Vivian's beliefs about the way her family saw her could be a little skewed came on her thirty-seventh birthday. Her sisters and parents came over to celebrate, and after a few glasses of wine, Vivian made a joke about her parents loving her sisters more because she had never really fit in.

Her mother's response stunned her.

"Vivi, we have always loved you and admired your independence," she said, "and we wanted to support you, but you always seemed to shut us out. I had to sneak into your room to find your drama schedule and then slip into the back of the auditorium so you wouldn't see me watching because I was afraid you didn't want me there."

And then her sisters chimed in.

"Yeah, Vi, you were always so much cooler than the rest of us. We thought you hated us."

Suddenly everything Vivian had believed about herself and her family all those years was thrown into a new light, and she realized it might be time to shift her paradigm.

She reached out to one of her closest friends for advice and began to see how this pattern of pushing people away had been playing out her whole life, and how it had been fueled by her fear of rejection.

Vivian was determined to do something about it, starting with her family. She began scheduling regular "sister nights," when the three of them would go out for dinner to chat and reconnect. Vivian couldn't believe how much fun they had together—how much she had been missing all those years she had held them at arm's length.

She also began working a little harder to connect with her coworkers, and even worked up the courage to ask if she could join them for happy hour. She was amazed when they told her that they assumed she hated them, which is why they never asked. And through her new connections, she learned of professional opportunities she otherwise would have missed.

Slowly Vivian began to let go of her belief that people can't be trusted and let herself be more vulnerable and connected to others. She still gets her feelings hurt every now and then, but overall, Vivian feels happier and more accepted than ever before.

Need more tips for moving past the fear of rejection and resisting the tendency to push other people away? Be sure to read chapters 11, 18, and 21!

chapter five

the self-doubter

When you're most afraid that you're not enough

> The moment you doubt whether you can fly, you cease forever to be able to do it.
>
> *J. M. Barrie, "Peter Pan"*

Sandra has always wondered what it would be like to feel confident.

Sometimes she looks at her three siblings, who seem to have all the confidence in the world, and wishes she could have just a tiny drop of whatever it was that they got. They have rewarding careers, seem to travel all the time, and are always living life to the fullest, while Sandra feels like she is simply sitting on the sidelines.

It's hard not to feel just a little resentful.

It hasn't always been this way, at least not completely. In high school, she was an athlete—the star of the volleyball team. She led her team to multiple state championships and was honored as the MVP.

Even so, deep down, she never felt like she was good enough. She was terrified that at some point people would start to notice she wasn't as good as everyone thought she was. In fact, the real reason she practiced so much—almost nonstop—was that she was always worried about falling short and failing to live up to everyone else's expectations.

She was offered a full-ride scholarship to play volleyball at a Division I school, but she turned it down, opting for community college instead, where she decided not to play. She just couldn't stand the pressure anymore.

But all these years later, she still wonders, *What if . . .?*

After college, Sandra got a job working as an executive assistant to the top sales manager at a local start-up. While it was challenging at first, and she spent the first year or so terrified she was going to mess something up and get fired, she eventually grew to love it. She always knew exactly what to do and how to handle every situation, and it was a *lot* of fun.

Eventually, though, she got married and soon thereafter got pregnant. At her husband's urging, she quit the job she loved to become a stay-at-home mom. Her three kids are older now and more independent, and while she loves her kids more than life itself, a part of her has always felt just a little bitter about having to give up her career.

Sandra loves her husband, but sometimes she makes fun of the way he dresses and does his hair, and she often comments on the fact that he works too much and has put on a few extra pounds over the past couple of years. He feels like she is way too critical, and when they fight, that's what he tells her.

Sandra knows she needs to lay off the criticism, but sometimes she just can't help herself. Sometimes it feels like it boils up inside, but she knows it has more to do with her unhappiness with herself than it does with anyone else. The reality is that Sandra's husband isn't the only one who has put on a few extra pounds. She knows she has too, and yet she can't seem to get her eating under control.

Sandra doesn't have a lot of close girlfriends, and she is often wistful of other women who do. Even so, she can't quite bring herself to open up in that way. Not long ago, her husband struck up a friendship with a guy at work, and his wife, Darcy, attempted to befriend Sandra as well. The four of them had dinner together one time, but after that, Sandra made excuses every time Darcy reached out.

The truth was that Sandra was completely intimidated by Darcy. She was beautiful, in great shape, ran her own personal training business, knew how to cook like a gourmet chef, and seemed to make friends wherever she went. She was everything Sandra wanted to be but was not.

And so, instead of opening up to her, Sandra became increasingly critical of Darcy—often making snarky comments to her husband about the way she dressed, her parenting style, and anything else she could think of. When Darcy and her husband decided to move away, the two couples met for one last time at a restaurant, where Sandra finally let down her guard and enjoyed a true heart-to-heart talk with Darcy. Only then did Sandra realize that her insecurity had caused her to miss out on what might have been a wonderful friendship.

Sandra is a Self-Doubter.

THE SELF-DOUBTER™ ARCHETYPE

Often plagued by a deep, sometimes hidden feeling of insecurity, the Self-Doubter struggles most with the fear of not being capable, which often manifests itself as the fear of not being good enough, whether "good" means smart enough, talented enough, educated enough, pretty enough, strong enough, well-spoken enough, cool enough, or any other number of *enoughs*.

Because Self-Doubters are frequently worried about being qualified or capable, they can be crippled by insecurity and uncertainty to the point that they're unable or unwilling to take any action at all.

The Self-Doubter constantly hears a voice in the back of her head that whispers things such as, "You can't do this," or "You're not capable," or "What makes you think you can do something like that?" This voice causes the Self-Doubter to constantly question her self-worth and to put herself down.

Interestingly, Self-Doubters sometimes try to hide or compensate for this insecurity by being hypercritical and judgmental of others. They project their own feelings of not being worthy onto people around them—particularly the people closest to them—who may be taking risks, going after their goals and dreams, or putting themselves out there in some way. As a result, Self-Doubters can sometimes come across as snarky or sarcastic.

Self-Doubters may also struggle with feelings of intense jealousy toward people who are doing the things they wish they could do if they weren't so afraid of not being capable. Again, this jealousy may manifest itself in the form of sarcasm, gossip, or criticism.

This propensity toward jealousy and criticism—which ultimately comes from a place of feeling unworthy—can have an adverse effect on relationships. Ironically, others close to the Self-Doubter may feel like they can never measure up to the Self-Doubter's expectations, which causes them to pull away. This, in turn, reinforces the Self-Doubter's belief that she is not good enough.

It's a vicious cycle.

Because the Self-Doubter harbors a deep feeling of insecurity, she is often hungry for praise and reassurance, sometimes insatiably so. The Self-Doubter craves validation and needs to hear frequent words of affirmation in order to build up her feelings of self-worth.

The Self-Doubter is the fifth most common fear archetype, with 3 percent of people showing this as their top archetype, and 24 percent having this archetype in their top three.

POSITIVE ATTRIBUTES

The Self-Doubter can be humble, self-effacing, and unpretentious. She is generally not boastful or prideful and does not have an overinflated ego. The Self-Doubter is often an exceptionally hard worker, always willing to put in extra effort, if only to compensate for any internally perceived weaknesses.

The Self-Doubter tends to be quite sensitive, and although she sometimes comes across as critical, she is usually empathetic and kind and very concerned with how others feel. The Self-Doubter is generally drawn to jobs that are laid out with a clear set of instructions and expectations, or to careers that allow for mastery of a very specific task.

AT A GLANCE
The Self-Doubter

- Is plagued by insecurity and feelings of not being good enough
- Is often paralyzed by self-doubt, which results in feeling stuck
- Is critical of others as a way to mask insecurity
- Is a very hard worker and will go above and beyond to do a good job
- Can be kind and empathetic and a good listener
- Is often humble and unpretentious

HABITS AND BEHAVIORS

- Is deeply afraid of not being capable and frequently feels unworthy
- Struggles with negative self-talk—a voice in the back of her head that makes her question her self-worth
- Frequently feels unqualified and "not enough"—not smart enough, educated enough, pretty enough, organized enough, and so on
- Has a tendency to be hypercritical of herself and others
- Can come across as negative or sarcastic

- Struggles with feelings of jealousy, especially toward those who are doing things she would like to do
- Craves reassurance and positive affirmation
- Tends to be humble and self-effacing; doesn't struggle with a large ego
- Sometimes has difficulty establishing or maintaining friendships
- Is often an exceptionally hard worker
- Can feel paralyzed or stuck due to insecurity
- Thinks, *Oh, I wouldn't know how to do that*, when asked to do something new
- Feels other people are more deserving of success
- Wishes for something better but doesn't believe herself capable of taking the necessary action required for change

THE VOICE OF THE SELF-DOUBTER

Here are some of the thoughts and beliefs expressed by survey respondents who received a high Self-Doubter score:

- "I don't set goals because I have no clue what I want, as I've spent my whole life learning to blend in. The words of my mother and ex-husband play over and over in my head that I'm not good enough and I'll never be good at anything."
- "I let fear hold me back from being a leader at church. I listened to the voices in my head tell me I wasn't good enough, that I didn't have enough time, that I didn't know enough to teach others about God, and that others would be able to see right through me. I let myself overthink everything and criticized myself. I backed out and then had to deal with the guilt of letting people down."
- "I'm afraid I'm going to fail because I always do. I just go till it gets too hard and then I quit. So why try?"

- "I detest public speaking or public attention of any kind. There are times when I've been asked to speak but have felt unqualified and inadequate. But then, after deciding not to step out of my comfort zone, I felt ashamed and disappointed in myself."
- "I'm so sure I'm going to fail that I don't even bother. Plus, I'm sure other people would wonder why I even tried because it was obvious I wouldn't succeed."
- "I am afraid to realize that I am not capable of what I really want to do and that no one will take me seriously or care about what I have to offer."
- "I know I have an athlete inside of me, but I just can't seem to act on it. It frustrates me and makes me so very sad. I want to just go out and do it, but I cannot seem to push through that insurmountable wall."
- "Everyone in my family is so smart, and I feel like the dumb one who always makes mistakes and never learns from them."
- "I'm so afraid of looking dumb or incompetent, and I always feel like I don't deserve the success or the position that I have, and that I am going to be exposed as an imposter."
- "For several years, I was afraid of leaving a job that was draining me. Because I didn't feel successful at the job, I didn't think I was capable of anything else. Instead of just viewing the job as maybe not a good fit, I thought there was something wrong with me. It kept me stuck for a very, very long time."

HOW THIS FEAR ARCHETYPE CAN HOLD YOU BACK

As a Self-Doubter, you struggle with a little voice in the back of your head that causes you to doubt your own abilities by telling you that you are not enough.

Here are some ways that being a Self-Doubter can adversely affect you and hold you back:

- You often avoid taking risks or trying new things because you worry that you don't have what it takes to be successful in the endeavor.
- You may find yourself frequently second-guessing your decisions or changing your mind out of fear that you can't do it.
- Instead of feeling happy for them, you often feel depressed or jealous when you see other people being successful, especially when they're successful doing something you would like to do but haven't dared to try.
- You may sabotage your relationships by becoming hypercritical of the people closest to you, making them feel like they can never live up to your expectations.
- You may be susceptible to peer pressure or to going along with a popular idea because you don't feel worthy or capable of speaking up.
- You may struggle with giving yourself or others grace and have a very hard time giving yourself the freedom to try new things and make mistakes.
- You may experience anxiety and fear when you are forced into a situation where you need to take a risk or step outside of your comfort zone, and you don't believe you possess enough of the required skills.
- You may let your own limiting beliefs about your abilities dictate what you allow yourself to do and what you think you're capable of.

STRATEGIES TO OVERCOME THIS FEAR

Here are a few strategies you can use to overcome your fear of not being good enough.

Reframe

As a Self-Doubter, you may feel down about yourself when something doesn't go quite right or when you make a mistake or experience failure. But it's important to remember that mistakes and failure are just a normal part of life. Plus, it's often our mistakes that teach us all the good stuff we need to know to keep moving forward!

Does that mean it's fun to make mistakes or to have things go wrong? No, of course not, and obviously the goal is to have things go right. But you can't let failure hold you back from going for it or from trying new things, because mistakes and failures are a different kind of win.

When you make a conscious choice to stop worrying about all the ways you might screw up and focus instead only on what you can learn from the experience, you give yourself the power to simply *try*, regardless of what the outcome will be. It takes away all the pressure to get it exactly right the first time and instead lets you fully enjoy the journey.

Take Action

Action is the antidote to fear, and for the Self-Doubter, the only way to truly overcome your insecurities and fears of not being capable is to start proving to yourself that you actually *are* capable.

The good news is that by taking small risks and small steps outside of your comfort zone, you'll eventually be able to work up the courage to take larger risks and larger steps outside of your comfort zone. Nothing builds up confidence faster than just taking action and doing it scared. So keep practicing, and do at least one thing that scares you every day.

Create Accountability

For the Self-Doubter, that little voice inside your head telling you that you're not capable can become so loud that it drowns out any counter-opinion. When that happens, it's easy to get lost in your own world of insecurity and inadequacy, even when those thoughts might not be based in reality. If you are struggling to combat those self-defeating thoughts and feelings of not being good enough, call for reinforcements by getting an outside perspective from a trusted friend, mentor, counselor, or coach.

Of course, this will mean making yourself vulnerable, and for the Self-Doubter, this can be the hardest part of all. Even so, hearing someone else tell you that your thoughts may not be accurate can make a huge difference. Even more importantly, a skilled coach or mentor can show you how to take steps to move past those fears and insecurities.

MOVING PAST INSECURITY

It was Sandra's intense regret over her experience with Darcy that ultimately convinced her that she needed to find a way to overcome her crippling self-doubt before it destroyed her. She began by reading a few self-help books and listening to motivational podcasts, and while those were helpful and somewhat inspiring, she also realized she might need some help to overcome the insecurity that had been welling up inside of her for so long.

Not comfortable talking to anyone she knew personally, she made an appointment with a life coach she found online. Her coach encouraged her to start by being more intentional about practicing self-care and to do a few things that were just for her, such as getting a gym membership, working out with a personal trainer, and joining a recreational volleyball league.

Sandra was amazed at how much fun she had playing volleyball again, especially now that she no longer felt the pressure to be the best. As she became more active and got in better shape, she also started feeling more confident about her appearance, which in turn made her feel a whole lot happier.

It was a difference that people really noticed, especially Sandra's husband and kids.

Sandra's life coach also encouraged her to push past her comfort zone and to consider going back to work. It took Sandra almost six months to work up the courage to start applying, but she eventually found a great part-time admin job that was both challenging and flexible.

But it was the newfound friendships that meant the most to Sandra. Instead of feeling jealous and unworthy around other women, she started to see their good qualities, and she began to realize she could appreciate the gifts in others without feeling inadequate about herself.

It was a huge shift, and one that has made all the difference.

 *do it scared*

Need more tips for moving past the fear of not being capable and for combating insecurity and feelings of inadequacy? Be sure to read chapters 10, 12, 14, and 19!

chapter six

the excuse maker

When you're most afraid of taking responsibility

> It is easier to move from failure to success than from excuses to success.
>
> *John C. Maxwell,*
> *Success 101*

Caroline is one of those people who makes a great first impression.

Smart, confident, and articulate, she's someone people really listen and look up to. It doesn't hurt that she always seems incredibly knowledgeable—she is clearly well-read and can often explain the theory or philosophy behind any number of thought leaders in her field.

In fact, she's so good at explaining other people's ideas that no one usually notices that Caroline is careful not to share her own thoughts and opinions or to say anything that could later be used against her.

Caroline has learned that it is safer to hide behind other people's ideas than to share her own and risk being blamed for them if they don't work out. Because she *hates* being on the hook.

As she grew up, Caroline's parents had extremely high expectations of her, and they put a lot of pressure on her to get good grades and to excel in music and sports.

That said, they also made a lot of excuses anytime she didn't live up to those expectations. More than once, they called her teachers to get her grade changed if she performed poorly on a test or report, even if the reason she performed poorly was that she hadn't studied. They insisted that the reason she didn't make the all-county orchestra was that they couldn't afford private lessons with the director, not because she hadn't done all that well on her audition.

Caroline learned that as long as she had some sort of justification for why she fell short, her parents wouldn't be disappointed in her.

In college, Caroline learned early on that the key to good grades in any course was just knowing how to mirror the thoughts and opinions of the professor teaching it. She got very good at knowing how to repeat back on her exams the exact words and phrases they used during lectures. As a result, she was always well-liked, and most of the time she got straight A's.

But every once in a while, a professor caught on to this strategy and would push her to articulate her own ideas. That was when Caroline really struggled, sometimes to the point that she dropped the class in order to avoid being pinned down.

After graduation, Caroline was hired as a project manager in the corporate office of a large manufacturing company. Adept at always knowing the right thing to say, she quickly made a name for herself within her department and was repeatedly promoted over the next number of years, eventually being named vice president of operations.

But it was in that role, at the top of her department, that Caroline began to struggle. Up to that point, she had always been asked to weigh in on decisions, but it was almost always someone else who made the final call. She never had to worry that she would be blamed for a bad decision or called out for making the wrong choice.

She *hated* being the one responsible.

In fact, it's why she eventually decided to walk away from her corporate job to become a consultant. She realized that she liked giving advice and enjoyed identifying options and presenting a number of viewpoints and thoughts to consider while never having to make the final decision. She liked staying on top of what was happening in the industry, but she never wanted to be the one at fault.

This tendency has carried over to her personal life as well. In her marriage and her friendships, she never wants to be the one to make the decision, whether it's which house to buy or what movie to see. And when she and her husband fight, his most frequent complaint is that she always seems to have an excuse for everything.

Caroline is an Excuse Maker.

THE EXCUSE MAKER™ ARCHETYPE

Also known as the Blame Shifter, the Excuse Maker archetype struggles most with the fear of taking responsibility, which can also manifest itself as the fear of being held accountable, or the fear of being found at fault.

Because the Excuse Maker is terrified of having the finger pointed in her direction, she frequently looks for an excuse—someone or something to blame—for why she can't do something or why her circumstances are what they are.

Often these reasons and rationalizations appear to be completely valid, which can sometimes make it hard to pin down the fact that the Excuse Maker is shifting blame and avoiding responsibility.

The Excuse Maker is extremely adept at diverting focus and attention away from herself and her own culpability to other people or circumstances. She is a masterful rationalizer, always seeming to have a reason or explanation for why she couldn't accomplish something.

The Excuse Maker can be uncomfortable in a leadership role and tends to get nervous at the idea of being in charge, taking risks, or putting herself in the line of fire, instead preferring to defer to the judgment of others. When it comes to making changes in her life or pursuing goals, the Excuse Maker usually—though not always—prefers to follow the example or guidance of someone else, such as a mentor, coach, or teacher. She pays close attention to what has worked for others and tries to follow suit.

The Excuse Maker tends to get uncomfortable when she is put on the spot or asked to share her opinion or thoughts, for fear of being held to that opinion or blamed for an unfavorable outcome. Indeed, she will often wait to share her own thoughts until others have shared their viewpoints and will often defer to someone else's judgment rather than take her own stance.

Ironically, the very nature of the Excuse Maker archetype—the tendency to avoid taking responsibility or to make excuses—makes it one of the more difficult archetypes to own and accept because this archetype's default tendency is to make excuses that deflect culpability.

That's why it's important to remember that the Excuse Maker archetype is *no better or worse* than the other fear archetypes. The reality is that none of the archetypes are positive; instead, they all hold us back in some way. And what's more, all of us have at least a little bit of every single one of the archetypes at work within us.

The Excuse Maker is the sixth most common fear archetype, with 3 percent of people showing this as their top archetype, and 20 percent having this archetype in their top three.

POSITIVE ATTRIBUTES

Excuse Makers can be excellent team players and are often great at collaborating and working with others. Because they are excellent learners and students of life, they are adept at assimilating lessons from the successes and mistakes of others. They also take direction well, and when paired with the right mentor or teacher, they can accomplish remarkable things.

Excuse Makers are good cheerleaders and are often very supportive of others. They have an ability to make other people feel and believe they are capable of doing great things. They also tend to be keen observers and have very good insight, even if they are sometimes reluctant to declare a strong opinion. Excuse Makers are happiest and most comfortable in strong supporting roles rather than direct leadership roles. They thrive in positions that allow them to ultimately defer to the judgment or opinion of someone above them.

AT A GLANCE
The Excuse Maker

- Tends to be fearful of taking responsibility or being blamed
- Makes excuses instead of progress
- Is hesitant to lead or take charge and prefers others to make decisions
+ Is often a good team player
+ Can be a skilled observer who learns from others' mistakes
+ Is often a great cheerleader

HABITS AND BEHAVIORS

- Is uncomfortable at the thought of taking the blame or shouldering responsibility for a mistake or error
- Frequently believes that her own setbacks and failures are the result of circumstances outside of her control or of others not doing their part
- Usually has an excuse or an explanation whenever something goes wrong; this excuse or explanation often appears completely valid and rational, and thus not easily identified as an excuse

- Is reluctant to share her own opinion for fear of being pinned down or held to that opinion
- Feels held back by a lack of guidance, support, or leadership, either currently or in the past (i.e., bad parents, a bad teacher, a bad boss, etc.)
- Sometimes attributes current struggles to things that happened long ago or in her childhood
- Often wishes for a teacher or guide to show her the way
- Struggles to make decisions in a group setting or on behalf of other people
- Prefers to work and collaborate with others rather than go out on her own

THE VOICE OF THE EXCUSE MAKER

Here are some of the thoughts and beliefs expressed by survey respondents who received a high Excuse Maker score:

- "Money is super tight right now, so that keeps me from moving forward with what I want to accomplish."
- "I'm nervous that if something goes wrong, everyone will be mad at me and I'll get blamed."
- "I've always dreamed of having my own little bakery business, but I can't do it financially. Student loans are a huge part of our debt, and there's no way I can see this dream coming true."
- "I am often overwhelmed at how much there is to learn and how little time I have before the bills are due to be paid. I need to earn money immediately, not six months from now."
- "I don't want to be the one responsible for everyone else."
- "I don't really have the time and resources to do it well, so I don't think I should do it at all."

- "My biggest dream in life is to be a horse trainer, but having little equestrian background at the age of twenty-two, I feel like I'm too old to begin my career in that field. It seems like all the successful horse trainers began before they could even walk. The whole prospect is very daunting to me, and it seems impossible."
- "I'd like to start my own business, but it feels like someone or something always stops me. I don't have time. I don't have money. There is no one to show me what to do."
- "I really want to write a book. I've always wanted to be a writer, and yet I never write. I always have an excuse. I know it's because I'm afraid, but I don't know how to push past that."
- "I'm afraid of having to do it alone and of having no support structure and no one to lean on."

HOW THIS FEAR ARCHETYPE CAN HOLD YOU BACK

The biggest danger the Excuse Maker archetype faces is an unwillingness to take full ownership of her life and of everything that happens to her. This default tendency to avoid being blamed or held responsible and to make excuses instead is really a way of giving up control of her own destiny. Because in the end, *even a good excuse is still just an excuse.*

Here are some ways being an Excuse Maker can adversely affect you and hold you back:

- You may struggle with making the final decision or conclusion if it's not a decision or conclusion someone else has come to first.
- It can be hard for you to voice your own thoughts and opinions, for fear of being held to those opinions later on.

- You can be uncomfortable taking the lead if it means you could be held responsible or blamed if something goes wrong.
- You are adept at coming up with good excuses or rationalizations for why you shouldn't attempt something or why you weren't able to accomplish something, even though in the end those excuses aren't serving you.
- Your tendency to make excuses or shift responsibility can be frustrating to others when it feels like you are unwilling to own your mistakes; this can adversely affect your relationships.
- You may experience anxiety, anger, or fear when you feel like you are being pinned down, blamed, or asked to take responsibility for a decision, and you may react by lashing out.
- You may struggle with taking risks.
- You may be prone to attribute current struggles or setbacks to things that happened in the past, such as a hard childhood, lack of support, or lack of a quality mentor. This prevents you from taking full responsibility in the present.

STRATEGIES TO OVERCOME THIS FEAR

Here are a few strategies you can use to help you move past your fear of taking responsibility.

Reframe

A big part of your fear comes from the script that has been playing inside your head—the message telling you that you don't want to take the blame. Thus, reframing the way you look at taking ownership and responsibility will help you move forward.

If deep down you believe that excuses will prevent you from ever being blamed, perhaps try telling yourself, "No one likes to hear excuses. People are much more likely to respect my work when I take responsibility." Likewise, if you're struggling with circumstances outside of your control, try telling yourself, "I may not have control over everything, but I can take responsibility for the choices I make."

Take Action

As an Excuse Maker, you may find that the most powerful action you can take in your life is to adopt a no-excuses mentality. It's an act of courage whenever you make the decision to accept responsibility for every choice and decision you make. A no-excuses mentality means putting an end to all the justifications and refusing to lay the blame on someone who hurt you, the circumstances you're in, or the terrible things that happened to you.

Psychologists refer to this concept as a shift in the locus of control, the extent to which people believe they have *internal* control over their lives, as opposed to believing that their lives are determined by *external* forces beyond their control. Not surprisingly, people who have an internal locus of control are far more motivated, productive, and successful in life. This means that becoming more motivated is often just a matter of taking responsibility for your choices.

While it may seem scary at first, adopting a no-excuses mentality and taking complete responsibility for your life and your circumstances are incredibly freeing! When you take ownership, you don't have to worry about what happens to you or how other people might treat you or what obstacles might come your way, because ultimately you are in control.

Create Accountability

It's never easy to have someone else point out your own tendency to make excuses, but there is probably no better way to overcome this particular fear than to actively seek out accountability, whether from a peer-to-peer accountability partner or from a teacher or mentor who embodies the qualities and skills you are hoping to develop.

Your accountability partner or mentor will be able to speak truth to you and let you know when you're making excuses, as well as when you're letting your fear of being blamed or taking responsibility hold you back. Ideally, you will find someone who isn't afraid to call you out and who will help you practice taking ownership and responsibility for your life and your decisions, one baby step at a time. It won't feel natural at first, but eventually, especially with the help of someone you admire and trust, you can get there.

MOVING PAST EXCUSES

Once Caroline started noticing how her pattern of making excuses and never wanting to take responsibility was adversely affecting her life and her relationships, she knew she needed to do something about it.

She hired a business coach to get more guidance and accountability, and her coach gradually helped her see some of the ways she had been avoiding responsibility or making excuses in her life and in her consulting business. It was hard at first for Caroline to accept that feedback and to take more ownership for her decisions, but as she practiced having a no-excuses mind-set, first for small decisions and then for larger ones, she began to feel a new sense of freedom and empowerment.

Her first really big breakthrough came when she was working with a consulting client. She had just presented several courses of action that the company could take, when the CEO turned to her and asked, "What do you think we should do?"

Normally, Caroline would have avoided answering the question by reiterating the options and explaining that she was there only to consult. But this time, Caroline looked the CEO straight in the eye and said, "If it were my company, I would absolutely pick option A, and that's what I think you should do."

The CEO agreed, thanked her for her advice, and then said, "And here I thought you were going to be one of those consultants who never actually gives their opinion."

Over time, Caroline came to realize that her clients would rather have her give real opinions that were sometimes wrong than wishy-washy advice that didn't help them make a decision. She learned that they respected her willingness to speak up and that they rarely held it against her when she got it wrong, as long as she was willing to own the mistake.

Slowly, taking ownership became easier and easier.

At home, Caroline's husband started noticing the shift as well, and he almost fell out of his chair the day Caroline said, "You know what, you're right! I shouldn't have done that, and I'm sorry. It was 100 percent my fault."

These days, Caroline keeps a sign above her desk that reads "No Excuses"—a continual reminder to take full responsibility for the choices she makes. She sees now how trapped she had been by her fear of being blamed, and she never wants to go back.

Need more tips for moving past the fear of taking responsibility and the need to make excuses? Be sure to read chapters 10, 11, and 20!

chapter seven

the pessimist

When you're most afraid of adversity

> You're only a victim to the degree of what your perception allows.
>
> *Shannon L. Alder*

Deep down, Janice feels like the deck has always been stacked against her. And while she wouldn't want to admit it to anyone, at this point, she often feels like she's just trying to survive without getting knocked down again.

Growing up, her family life was pretty dysfunctional, and she distinctly remembers wishing and praying that her family could just be normal. All her friends seemed to have perfect parents and perfect lives, while Janice's dad drank too much and her mom was always completely frazzled. While they weren't exactly poor, her parents always seemed stressed out about money, and they fought all the time.

Eventually, when Janice was in seventh grade, her parents divorced. Janice was so ashamed that she never told anyone, and she avoided inviting friends over so that no one would discover her secret.

She went to college and was doing okay until her sophomore year, when she came down with mono. For months, she had almost no energy and could barely make it to class. Her grades started slipping, and she ended up losing her scholarship. Without the scholarship, school was too expensive to continue, and she was forced to drop out.

After leaving school, she went to work full-time as a receptionist in an office. She thought she might have a chance to work her way up the corporate ladder, but after being passed up for two promotions because her boss clearly didn't like her, she decided to look for other options. She signed up for night classes at a local cosmetology school and trained to become an esthetician, and then she got a job working at a local hotel spa.

She discovered that she loved helping people solve their skin issues and that she was good at it. She developed a loyal client base, though sometimes she felt more like a therapist than an esthetician—people were always sharing all their relationship problems! Most of the time, Janice was a great listener, which is why people tended to open up.

After a few years of working at the spa, Janice and a couple of coworkers decided to strike out on their own and open a small massage and skin care clinic. Things went well for the first couple of years, but then Janice began noticing that her two business partners were becoming closer, and it felt like they were shutting her out. A couple of times, she caught them meeting without her and making decisions about the business without consulting her, and things began to get tense.

Then Janice went on a monthlong vacation to Europe—a trip she had been planning for years. Her partners were supposed to cover her clients while she was gone, but instead they hijacked the entire business and removed Janice as a partner.

Janice was devastated.

She cried for three days, not understanding how anyone could be so hurtful and selfish.

Eventually she went back to work for the hotel spa, but the bitterness and anger she felt made it hard to enjoy the work she was doing. Now when her clients share their problems, she can't help but roll her eyes when they aren't looking. If only they knew what *real* problems were!

At this point, Janice feels like she has tried hard to get ahead, but she just keeps getting pushed back down. What is the point of even trying when life is clearly so unfair? She's done putting herself out there and getting devastated in the process. It really doesn't feel like there is any good solution, and she's afraid of putting in the effort only to be betrayed or shot down. She's scared of adversity because it feels like her life has been nothing *but* adversity.

Janice is a Pessimist.

THE PESSIMIST™ ARCHETYPE

Often a casualty of circumstances outside her control, the Pessimist archetype struggles most with the fear of adversity, which often manifests itself as the fear of struggling through hard things, or the fear of pain.

Because the Pessimist has experienced some sort of hardship, tragedy, or adversity in her life, either recently or in the past, she has legitimate reason to feel victimized. But allowing herself to stay in that victim role is exactly what keeps the Pessimist stuck.

Because they are so afraid of adversity and hardship, and because they feel like they lack control over their situation, Pessimists are easily waylaid by any difficult or challenging circumstances that come their way. Instead of seeing obstacles as opportunities for growth and perseverance, Pessimists view their tragedies and hardships as legitimate reasons to give up or to not try at all.

Pessimists are often unable or unwilling to face their circumstances head-on, preferring instead to hide to avoid additional pain. Ironically, this response often makes things worse.

It can be difficult for the Pessimist to get perspective or to see beyond her own pain, hardship, and difficult circumstances. It may feel like everyone else has it easier or that she's gotten the short end of the stick. It's likely she also can't see her own victim-ness.

The Pessimist can sometimes come across as bitter, and she often feels she has been dealt a worse hand than other people, which leads her to think that life is fundamentally unfair. The Pessimist also believes she is a victim of her circumstances, and she feels she lacks control of her own destiny.

Not surprisingly, the very nature of the Pessimist fear archetype makes it one of the most difficult, if not *the* most difficult, archetype to own and accept. Indeed, the most common reactions to finding out one is a Pessimist are anger, denial, and taking offense. No one wants to see herself as a pessimist or a victim, even if that mentality is exactly what may be keeping her stuck.

It's good to remember here that the Pessimist archetype is *no better or worse* than the other fear archetypes. All of them hold us back in some way, and all of us have at least a little bit of every single archetype inside of us.

The Pessimist is the least common fear archetype, with 3.4 percent of people showing this as their top archetype, and 16.9 percent having this archetype in their top three.

POSITIVE ATTRIBUTES

Pessimists tend to be sensitive and bighearted. They are often told that they wear their heart on their sleeve and that they feel things more deeply and intensely than others do.

Because of this, they are usually incredibly caring, compassionate, and kind, and they also possess a lot of empathy for others. They are typically quite social, are good listeners, and can also be thoughtful and reflective.

Pessimists are often drawn to careers that put them in a position of caring for and interacting with other people, as well as careers that require thoughtfulness and creative expression. Common career paths include nursing, caregiving, social work, physical therapy, counseling, cosmetology, massage therapy, esthetics, art, teaching, and writing.

AT A GLANCE
The Pessimist

- ⊖ Fears adversity, yet often seems to be in the midst of it
- ⊖ Tends to see hardship as a stop sign rather than a stepping-stone
- ⊖ Feels powerless to change her circumstances and may become bitter
- ⊕ Tends to be caring and compassionate
- ⊕ Possesses a high level of empathy and is often a good listener
- ⊕ Is sensitive and bighearted

HABITS AND BEHAVIORS

- Frequently has trouble moving beyond difficult circumstances from the past
- Often feels like there is no solution to her problems
- Looks at hardships as stop signs rather than stepping-stones
- Tends to believe she has it worse than most people she knows
- Often feels that circumstances outside of her control stand in the way of her achieving her goals
- May shut down in the face of adversity or challenges
- Is likely to give up rather than push through when the going gets tough
- Tends to feel emotions more intensely than other people
- Can be sensitive to criticism and adversity

- Can sometimes get lost in her own thoughts
- Often avoids taking risks

THE VOICE OF THE PESSIMIST

Here are some of the thoughts and beliefs expressed by survey respondents who received a high Pessimist score:

- "I'm worried that what I want to do will be too hard."
- "I don't want to waste all that time and effort only to get shot down yet again."
- "My first pregnancy was fraught with difficulty. My doctor didn't listen to me, and I was uncomfortable under his care, but no one listened. I did not change providers, and my baby died during labor. I wish I had spoken up and followed my intuition. I have been devastated by her loss ever since."
- "The thing that holds me back is *life*—I've had cancer; I've had to take care of my elderly parents; my family never has any money. There are things I would like to do, but it's just not possible."
- "I'm so tired of trying and failing. I just don't want to do it anymore."
- "I'm afraid of adding extra work and time when I'm always tired, not knowing if it will be worth it in the end. It's exhausting being the main breadwinner and the wife and mom. I rarely have time to do anything fun for myself with a special needs child who can't ever be left alone—even as a teenager. Not to mention my elderly parents and my neglected house."
- "After a car accident ended my dance career and the economy crashed at the same time, I was left with a pile of issues. I couldn't run the company because of injuries. I could no longer dance because of injuries. I was stuck not knowing

which direction to go or how to move forward in life. It froze me in time for years and still holds me back in many ways."

- "I don't want to give my husband more ammunition. He doesn't believe in me, so that makes me think I can't do it."
- "I always try new things, but old problems always get in the way and drag me down."

HOW THIS FEAR ARCHETYPE CAN HOLD YOU BACK

Perception is reality, and for the Pessimist archetype, the feeling that life isn't fair or that you've had it worse than others can be crippling. Often this feeling or perception comes from genuinely difficult circumstances—tragedy, illness, betrayal, or loss—that you're struggling to move past.

It's important to know that the pain, anger, and bitterness you feel are legitimate and perhaps even warranted. That said, allowing yourself to stay stuck as a result of difficult circumstances is not serving you and may in fact be holding you back. Here are some ways that being a Pessimist can adversely affect you and keep you stuck:

- You tend to get easily discouraged and have trouble fighting through challenges and adversity. Instead, you get stuck or frustrated in the "messy middle."
- You may sometimes get caught in a cycle of self-pity and a "poor me" mentality, believing that life is unfair or that circumstances have been worse for you than for other people. While this may or may not be accurate, feeling sorry for yourself is only holding you back.
- You may struggle with forgiveness and with giving other people grace when you feel you have been wronged.
- You may struggle to maintain positive relationships with people whom you perceive as having it better than

you. Your tendency to see life as unfair can cause you to be jealous of those you perceive as having been dealt a better hand.

- Your fear of pain and adversity may cause you to avoid taking risks—even small ones—or to avoid going after big goals and dreams because even the thought of struggle is very uncomfortable.
- You may experience anxiety and fear when you anticipate that something may be hard.
- You may allow set beliefs about the things that have happened to you, your life circumstances, or the way people have treated you in the past to dictate what you believe you are capable of.

STRATEGIES TO OVERCOME THIS FEAR

Here are a few strategies you can use to overcome your fear of adversity.

Reframe

Adversity is never fun. Illness, tragedy, abuse, betrayal, depression, financial difficulty, disappointments, mistakes, blunders, and hardships—the list of horrible things that can and do happen in life is almost endless. Most are things we wouldn't wish on our worst enemy.

Chances are you've already experienced an extreme amount of adversity, which has left you terrified of experiencing more. Even so, there is almost always something good that can come from tragedy or difficult circumstances. Instead of looking at hardships as stop signs, you can begin to look at them as stepping-stones to where you need to go.

No, it's not fun to make mistakes or to experience tragedy and hardship. But it's important not to let the fear of having to overcome adversity become the thing that holds you back from going for it or from trying new things.

A big part of your fear comes from the script that has been playing inside your head, and that means if you want to break this fear, you're going to have to start playing a new message. If deep down you believe you've been dealt a rotten hand, then what can you tell yourself that will help you start changing that view? Likewise, if you're dealing with anger or bitterness because of the way you've been treated, or if you've struggled with feeling like life isn't fair, then it's time to start rewriting the message you are playing inside your head.

Sometimes positive affirmations that you repeat to yourself will be enough. Other times it may mean finding more positive messages to listen to, such as those found on audiobooks or podcasts. It may mean seeking spiritual help through Scripture, worship, or a spiritual adviser. It may even require outside help from a therapist or counselor.

Take Action

A key indicator of the Pessimist archetype is feeling like you've had to deal with a whole lot of unfair or difficult circumstances that are completely outside your control. And while you can't always change your circumstances—what happens to you or how others treat you—you *can* change the way you choose to respond.

Like the Excuse Maker, the Pessimist needs to develop an internal locus of control. While it may seem scary at first, realizing you have the ability to say that no matter who hurt you or what terrible things happened, you still have a choice is incredibly liberating! When you take back control of your response, you don't have to worry about what happens to you or how other people may treat you or what obstacles may come your way, because ultimately, *it is still your life, and no one else's.*

Create Accountability

When you're dealing with tragedy, illness, or any sort of adversity, it can be hard to get perspective, to "see the forest for the trees." In the moment, it feels like the deck has been stacked against you—life just isn't fair and things for you are so much worse than they are for other people. But the reality is that while everyone's hardship and adversity look a little different, hardship and adversity happen to everyone. No one is immune, even if their battles happen behind closed doors. Take comfort in knowing that you are not alone, and actively seek out friends or accountability partners who can help give you that outside perspective.

Depending on the circumstances you're facing, you may even want to consider joining a support group—you can find them for everything from grief and substance abuse to depression, debt relief, and so much more. A support group can help you remember that others have already walked this path, and it may even offer solutions you haven't considered.

MOVING PAST PESSIMISM

Finally realizing she was sinking deeper and deeper into a hole of bitterness and anger, Janice decided to get some outside help. She started seeing a counselor, who helped her get more perspective on the childhood she had always seen as dysfunctional.

Janice began to realize that her parents, while certainly not perfect, had done the best they could and had also done a lot of things right. She began to have more compassion for the stress they both must have felt, and even had a heart-to-heart talk with her mom that shed a lot of light on circumstances she hadn't really understood as a child.

She also worked through her bitterness about being forced to drop out of college, and she was shocked to finally admit to herself that she hadn't really liked college that much and that the real reason her grades started slipping was that she wasn't interested in the classes she had been taking. She also realized that she really did love esthetics and that she couldn't imagine doing anything else for work.

For Janice, it felt like a load had been lifted, because now when she looked back on her college experience, she felt grateful that her bout with mono had helped her find a different path.

As far as her business partners were concerned, Janice still felt a lot of anger, but her counselor helped her see that bitterness was eating her up inside and was not serving her well. She decided to make a conscious choice to forgive them and move on. It wasn't easy, and for Janice it took a lot of time and a lot of prayer, but eventually the anger started to subside.

In the meantime, Janice threw herself into serving her clients at the hotel spa. She became the top esthetician on the team, was able to double her rates, and became the first to ever have her own waiting list. She was even awarded Employee of the Year by the hotel manager.

It took some deep work, but Janice now sees exactly how much her fear of adversity was holding her back, and she is determined to never again allow the circumstances she *can't* control to dictate the things she can.

Need more tips for moving past the fear of adversity and feelings of victimhood and for taking back control of your own destiny? Be sure to read chapters 10, 12, 14, and 20.

the fear archetypes at a glance

THE PROCRASTINATOR

Primary fear: Struggles most with the fear of making a mistake, which often manifests itself as perfectionism or the fear of commitment

Negative traits: Likes things to be "right" and spends too much time researching and planning; has trouble both getting started and feeling like things are finished

Positive attributes: Produces high-quality work; is usually well-organized and pays great attention to detail

THE RULE FOLLOWER

Primary fear: Struggles most with an outsized fear of authority, which often manifests itself as an irrational aversion to breaking the rules or doing something that is perceived as "not allowed"

Negative traits: Gets nervous about not doing something the way it's supposed to be done; may adhere to a rule or the status quo at the expense of own judgment

Positive attributes: Is extremely trustworthy and responsible; possesses a strong sense of duty and right and wrong

THE PEOPLE PLEASER

Primary fear: Struggles most with the fear of being judged, which also manifests itself as the fear of letting people down and the fear of what other people might say

Negative traits: Has trouble saying no and struggles to set boundaries; can be hesitant to take action, fearing what others may think

Positive attributes: Tends to be well-liked and fun to be around; is thoughtful, considerate, and generous; is a great team player

THE OUTCAST

Primary fear: Struggles most with the fear of rejection, or a fear of trusting other people—a fear that often manifests itself by rejecting others before one has a chance to be rejected

Negative traits: May outwardly appear to be fearless or unfazed by what others think; sometimes struggles as part of a team and may seek out risky or self-destructive behavior

Positive attributes: Is self-motivated and driven to succeed; tends to be persistent, willing to take risks, and not easily discouraged by failure

THE SELF-DOUBTER

Primary fear: Struggles most with the fear of not being capable, which often manifests itself as deep feelings of insecurity and the fear of not being good enough

Negative traits: Feels paralyzed by insecurity and therefore stuck; often critical of others as a way to mask insecurity

Positive attributes: Is a very hard worker who will go above and beyond to do a good job; can be kind, empathetic, humble, and a good listener

THE EXCUSE MAKER

Primary fear: Struggles most with the fear of taking responsibility, which can manifest itself as the fear of being held accountable, or the fear of being blamed

Negative traits: Often makes excuses instead of progress; can be hesitant to lead or take charge, preferring others to make decisions

Positive attributes: Is a good team player and an excellent cheerleader; can be a keen observer who learns from others' successes and mistakes

THE PESSIMIST

Primary fear: Struggles most with the fear of adversity, which can manifest itself as the fear of experiencing hardships and difficulties, or the fear of pain

Negative traits: Feels powerless to change circumstances; tends to see hardships as stop signs rather than stepping-stones

Positive attributes: Is sensitive and bighearted; tends to be caring and compassionate and is often a good listener

PART TWO

the principles of courage

Once you've identified the unique ways your own fear may be manifesting itself in your life, it's time to start moving past it. This process begins with changing your mind-set, as well as letting go of the limiting beliefs you may have about yourself and others.

Adopting a new set of principles—the Principles of Courage—can help you make this shift. These principles are designed to help you reframe your perceptions and provide a new set of core beliefs so you'll be equipped to face your fears, overcome obstacles, and create a life you love.

chapter eight

dare to think big

Because stretch goals are the secret to getting and staying motivated

| A good goal is like a strenuous exercise—it makes you stretch. | *Mary Kay Ash* |

Nine years ago, mostly on a whim, I founded what would eventually become my company, Ruth Soukup Omnimedia. Of course, at that point, it wasn't a company! Not even close. For starters, I had absolutely *no* idea what I was doing. I didn't even know that starting an online business—a virtual company—could be a thing, and I certainly wasn't trying to start one of my own.

At the time, I was a stay-at-home mom of two toddlers, looking for something to do. Truth be told, I was going a little stir-crazy, and most days the only thing I could think to do to get out of the house was to go to Target. And so we went to Target. A lot. And I spent a lot more than I should have. As a result, my husband and I started fighting about money. I desperately needed something to do that wasn't shopping, and I thought, *Why don't I start writing about trying to live well and spend less?* I figured that, if nothing else, starting a blog would give me something to do and also help keep me accountable.

But after I had been sharing my thoughts online for a few weeks, I quickly began to realize that there was this whole other world out there that I had never known about, a world of entrepreneurs and go-getters and online business owners. I discovered there were people—other stay-at-home moms even—who were actually making *real money* while they worked from home, and I decided I wanted to do that too.

And that's when I made this big, scary, totally *crazy* goal that I was going to make enough money through my fledgling online business—this little blog I had started—that my husband could quit his job.

I can't even tell you what an impossible goal this seemed like at that point. First of all, my husband was an aerospace engineer, so he was making pretty good money. It wasn't like he was working part-time at the local hardware store or something—this was a serious income I would need to replace. Second, at the time I set that goal, my business was making exactly $0, and I had about four readers, one of whom was me.

This wasn't just a big goal; this was an insane goal. A "the lady has lost her mind" kind of goal. And that's exactly what my husband said when I told him my plan. In fact, I think his exact words were, "Honey, that is the stupidest thing you have ever said. You can't make money on a blog." He wasn't trying to be mean or burst my bubble. It really did seem like a stupid, crazy, totally-out-of-the-realm-of-reasonable-possibilities kind of idea.

But you know what?

I didn't care.

The thing is, I had set other goals in my life, and I'd even had what I thought were pretty big goals—goals like getting into a top 20 law school—but this was the first time I'd ever had a goal so big that I had no idea how I would actually accomplish it. I had no idea how I was going to make it a reality, but I was committed to figuring it out.

And it didn't matter to me that my husband thought I was crazy. It didn't matter to me that my friends didn't get it, or that they made fun of me behind my back. It didn't matter to me that I had to work harder than I'd ever worked.

Once I was committed to this big goal, I was ready and willing to do whatever it took.

Yes, I was scared. Terrified, actually. And yes, I had absolutely no idea what I was doing. But I knew if I could just keep trying, I would figure it out eventually. I knew there had to be a way, even if I didn't know exactly what that way looked like.

WHY WE NEED STRETCH GOALS

On a recent business trip, I spent some time running on the treadmill in the workout room of the hotel where I was staying. When I was done but still in my workout clothes, I headed to the free breakfast buffet where, trying to be good, I picked out some hardboiled eggs, fresh strawberries, Greek yogurt, and walnuts.

The man behind me in line couldn't help but comment on my plate. "Wow, that looks *really* healthy."

It was clearly not meant as a compliment, but I just laughed and responded, "There's no point working out for an hour only to go and eat a waffle!"

To which he (somewhat snarkily) replied, "I think I'll take the waffle."

We continued to chat, and I explained that I had set a goal to be in the best shape of my life by my fortieth birthday. I had only seven weeks to go, so I had to be on top of it.

"It's good to have goals, I guess," he responded, "as long as they're realistic. I don't think you want to set goals that are too big."

In that moment, it took every ounce of willpower for me not to scream, "You don't know how *wrong* you are!"

I didn't, because it wasn't the time or the place to get into a giant debate with a random stranger. But the truth is, *I could not have disagreed more*!

We *need* big goals in our lives!

We need goals that motivate us and make our chest tighten or get those butterflies going in our stomach. Goals so big that they scare us a little but also invigorate us and get us more excited to jump out of bed in the morning. Big goals provide the road map for our lives, the compass that tells us we're moving in the right direction.

Big goals are the spark that lights the fire inside us!

Have you ever noticed that at the beginning of the year, we start out with the best intentions of what our year will look like? It's a fresh start, a clean slate, and so we make all sorts of resolutions—a whole list of all those things we want to accomplish.

But then, somewhere in mid-February, all that renewed energy we felt at the beginning of the year starts to fizzle out. Life gets in the way. The reality of all those day-to-day responsibilities starts to weigh us down, and we don't feel quite as enthusiastic. We lose focus. We work on one thing one day and another thing another day, and we never really gain enough traction in any one area to feel like we've accomplished something.

Why?

I believe it's because we need *big* goals to actually get *big* things done.

And that's exactly why this is the first principle of courage: **Dare to think big.**

Over the past few years, the most important thing I've learned about overcoming fear and setting effective, life-changing goals is that setting a whole bunch of smaller goals that *seem* like they should be attainable is counterproductive to getting big results.

Have you ever heard of SMART goals? I'm guessing yes, as it is the reigning conventional wisdom when it comes to goal setting. It's basically the idea that your goals should be **S**pecific, **M**easurable, **A**ttainable, **R**elevant, and **T**ime Bound. Meaning you should know exactly what you are trying to do; your goal should be quantifiable in some way; it should be something you can actually accomplish; it should be meaningful to you; and it should have a deadline.

While this SMART goal framework seems very practical—and it is, I guess, in some ways—in all its practicality, it leaves out the most important part of setting goals, the part that will actually *get* and *keep* you motivated.

The most important part is *thinking big* and creating a stretch goal—one that pushes us past our comfort zone or one we might not fully believe is attainable, at least not for us. It's daring to believe we are capable of more and daring to push ourselves past our current limits to create something amazing. It's daring to set goals so big they scare us. Goals that make our chest tighten or our stomach flutter.

Those are the goals that will motivate us.

You see, when we set goals that feel safe and achievable, we are caving in to our own preconceived notions of what we are capable of. We're not pushing past our comfort zone; we're just settling for the status quo. And there is nothing inherently motivating about that. It's comfortable. It's what we know. It doesn't require us to stretch or change or work any harder than we already are. And so we don't. In fact, sometimes—often—we work less hard. We do the bare minimum. We get bored and lose focus.

But when we set—and commit to—a big goal, one so big it freaks us out a little, we force ourselves out of that comfort zone into the unknown. Is it scary? Yes! But it is also totally invigorating and completely motivating. There's nothing that will make us work harder or keep us going longer.

The reality is that the flutter in our stomach and the tightening in our chest is *fear*, but it's the *good* kind of fear—the kind of fear that kicks in when we need to do things we don't think we can do.

And if you don't feel that way toward your goals? Then I would dare say your goals aren't big enough! And I'd challenge you to start thinking bigger and pushing yourself just a little bit harder.

ELIMINATE SELF-JUDGMENT

Of course when it comes to thinking bigger about your goals, the very first step you'll need to take is to give yourself permission to start visualizing all the possibilities. And by that, I mean you need to give yourself the freedom to dream big without self-editing or self-judgment.

And to be perfectly honest, for most people, this is the hardest part.

We're often so critical of ourselves and so afraid to actually dream about the possibilities. We tell ourselves our dreams are stupid . . . before we've even had a chance to dream them.

Or it could be that we're just so bogged down in the realities of life, the place we're at right at this very moment—with all the responsibilities, limitations, frustrations, and obstacles—that we can't allow ourselves to imagine, even for just a few minutes, that things could possibly be different. In our mind, the current reality is our only reality.

But it's not! There is a whole world of possibilities out there, an infinite number of doors waiting to be opened and explored, and the only limit on what you are capable of, no matter where you're at in life right now, is your willingness to dream bigger and then put your head down and get to work.

So give yourself permission to dream *big* without judgment or self-editing, and start asking yourself important, thought-provoking questions like these:

- What have I always wanted to do?
- What am I interested in or passionate about that I've never dared to pursue?
- What would I do if nothing stood in my way?
- What motivates me or gets me excited to jump out of bed in the morning?
- What did I dream about doing before life got in the way?

- Where would I like to see myself five years or ten years from now?
- What would be the ultimate dream life for me? What does it look like?

Make a conscious choice, even if just for a few minutes, to turn off all those voices in your head that instantly tell you that's not possible or that's stupid or "who are you to even think about something like that?" Just turn them off and dream. Don't hold back. Don't worry about what's possible or impossible. Don't worry about how you'll get there. Don't self-edit. Allow yourself to imagine the wildest possibilities, even if they are completely crazy and unrealistic.

Give yourself permission to think big.

WANTING TO WANT SOMETHING

And while this may sound so easy in theory, I know that in practice the idea of big goals is really, really hard for a lot of people (and *especially* for moms!). I talk to so many friends who tell me they've spent so much time taking care of everyone else around them that they feel like they've lost themselves in the process. They don't even really know what they want, or what they should want.

In fact, just a few months ago, a friend shared that she might be depressed because she just felt so *purposeless*. For the past fourteen years, she had poured herself into being a mom, but now her kids were getting older and more independent, and she had no idea what to do with herself, or even who she really was, aside from "Mom."

"I want to do something that matters," she said, "something I care about. I see all these other women doing all these really cool things, but I just have no idea what my thing should be."

Another friend put it succinctly when she told me, "I just want to want something."

What I realized later is that just that very statement *is* a big goal! In fact, it's a huge goal—perhaps the biggest one of all. Daring to discover your purpose is definitely not for the faint of heart.

But if you've ever found yourself saying something similar, it may just mean that figuring out exactly who you are and what it is you want is the big goal you need to be working on right now. It may mean taking some time for yourself—planning a personal retreat or a day or two away just to think. It may mean journaling or reading books related to a few topics you're interested in. It may mean taking a class or attending a lecture. It may mean going to counseling or even hiring a life coach.

But first you'll have to see it as a big goal—perhaps the biggest of your life—and commit to it accordingly.

ACTION IS THE ANTIDOTE TO FEAR

Of course, once you've identified this big goal of yours, there is another critical step to take—you'll need to take action and execute. A goal is nothing without action, and no matter how scary or impossible your big goal may seem in the beginning, I guarantee that taking action—any action, however small—is the quickest way to overcome your hesitation. Remember, *action is the antidote to fear.*

Taking action means you'll need to rearrange your schedule and put your big goal *first* every single day, and then start doing whatever it takes to make your big goal a reality. It may mean getting up earlier every day. It may mean saying no to other, lesser opportunities and distractions that will get in the way of achieving your big goal. It may sometimes mean saying no to things you really want to do.

It could mean taking a class or going back to school, looking for another job, or taking some other kind of risk. It may mean making a financial investment in supplies or training or travel. It should definitely mean blocking out time each week—and maybe even every day—to get yourself one step closer to the finish line.

And it will certainly mean digging deep to keep going when the road gets rough or when obstacles stand in your way, and developing grit and a thick skin for when people don't understand. But once you're fully committed to making your big goal a reality, these things won't feel like a burden or an imposition. You'll do them willingly, knowing that the road won't always be easy, but it will be worth it.

For me, as I was getting my business off the ground, putting my big goal first meant getting up at 3:00 a.m. every single day, even on the weekends, so I could find time to work on this budding start-up and still be a mom. It meant learning everything I could about creating an online business, and constantly trying new things to see what would work, often failing nine times out of ten. It meant stepping *way* outside of my comfort zone to attend conferences and seek out new opportunities and even to make goofy YouTube videos of my coupon-shopping adventures. It meant sacrificing a lot of free time and fun time and friend time.

But to me, it was always worth it, even if it wasn't always fun or comfortable in the moment. And in the end, those sacrifices paid off in ways I never could have begun to imagine. In 2013, two and a half years after I started my business on a whim, my husband was able to quit his job, and that original crazy, impossible goal became a reality, paving the way for even bigger and crazier goals.

But even if it hadn't happened that way, I don't think I would have been sorry for all the sacrifices I made, or for the ones I continue to make even to this day—not even for a minute. I would have been *really* proud of trying. And the truth is that most of the joy in my journey so far has come from the struggle, from the challenges I've had to work through and obstacles I've had to overcome.

Because those big goals—even when we don't fully achieve them—are what make life worth living! *They* are the things that spark our passion and get us excited to jump out of bed in the morning! *They* are the things that keep us going, even in the dull moments or the hard moments or the painful moments.

Those big goals—the ones we have to stretch and push and fight for—are what empower us to create a life we *love*, not just one we tolerate.

So do it. Dare to think *big*.

Because stretch goals are the secret to getting and staying motivated.

chapter nine

rules are for suckers

Because you should never be afraid to think for yourself

When you grow up you tend to get told that the world is the way it is and your life is just to live your life inside the world. Try not to bash into the walls too much. Try to have a nice family life, have fun, save a little money. That's a very limited life. Life can be much broader once you discover one simple fact, and that is—everything around you that you call life was made up by people that were no smarter than you. And you can change it, you can influence it . . . Once you learn that, you'll never be the same again.
Steve Jobs

Rules are for suckers.

It sounds so rebellious, doesn't it?

The funny thing is that this little mantra of mine started out as a joke. My husband and I were discussing some story in the news—I can't remember the details anymore—but it was another story about someone who had broken all the rules and not only had gotten away with it but had actually come out ahead. They had won *because* they broke the rules.

"Oh, honey," I said, "don't you know that rules are for suckers?"

We both laughed and then moved on to the next topic of conversation. But a short time later, it came up again. Another news story. Another person breaking the rules and coming out ahead. Another example of how thinking outside the box is the key to success.

Over and over again, I found myself saying it: "Rules are for suckers."

Eventually I started to embrace it. Because the thing is, I think I've known it for a while.

You see, when I was in my early twenties, I went through a terrible, completely debilitating depression. I attempted suicide several times, and my worst attempt landed me in a coma on life support with a less than 10 percent chance of waking up. I was a mess.

And during that depression, I spent more than *two years* in and out of psychiatric hospitals. I had lost all hope and all meaning.

But during that time, I also lost all concept of what it meant to play by the rules.

Most of the time, we all operate within a set of established norms. We talk a certain way, dress a certain way, follow instructions, and self-edit and self-regulate. We don't dare rock the boat. We pay attention to what everyone else is doing and try to keep our own behavior in line. In short, most of us are rule followers, whether we realize it or not.

But when I found myself in that mental hospital for the first time, the still-sane part of me recognized that I had gone off the deep end and that suddenly the rules didn't apply anymore. In fact, at the hospital, patients walked around in bathrobes, rocked in the corner, publicly swore and sulked and cried, and sometimes even threw chairs just for the fun of it. Crazy people do not fit within the established norms. And once I had joined the Land of Insanity, I didn't have to worry about what everyone else was doing.

In a scary sort of way, it was strangely liberating.

While I've long since recovered from that depression, and while it has been more than fifteen years since I reentered the world of "normal" people, that lesson is one that has stuck with me.

Rules are for suckers. And that's the second principle of courage.

In fact, it's even a principle I teach my kids, which a lot of people tell me is completely nuts. "What are you going to do when that backfires and they stop listening to you?" they ask.

And truthfully, I'm just waiting for the day the principal calls because one of my kids (and I'm pretty sure it will be my younger daughter) decided to share this little philosophy of life at the wrong time. So allow me to clarify.

What I'm *really* teaching my kids is not that *all* rules are stupid. I tell them there are lots of really good rules out there. Important rules we *should* follow. But there are also a lot of dumb rules out there, rules that make no sense, rules that other people made up just to make themselves feel important or because things have always been done that way or because they made sense at the time but don't anymore.

What I want them to develop is a healthy skepticism and a willingness to question authority and the status quo. I never want them to just follow blindly because someone told them it was a rule. I want them to know it's okay to follow their own path.

EMBRACE COMMON SENSE

By now you may have noticed this simple fact: just because someone says something is true, or because it shows up on the internet, or because "everyone" is repeating it as fact doesn't *actually* make it true.

That's where good old-fashioned common sense and critical thinking skills are so important. The next time you hear something that "everyone" is talking about—or freaking out over—ask yourself, *Does this actually make sense? Is this the crisis or emergency people are making it out to be? Could there be a different perspective?*

I don't know about you, but I feel like the rise of the internet and social media has had a direct correlation with the loss of common sense. In so many different areas of our lives, there is this Chicken Little "sky is falling" mentality about, well, practically everything.

When I was pregnant with my first daughter, I joined an online forum called BabyFit, a place where thousands of expectant moms—most of us first-time moms—came to discuss all things pregnancy and childbirth related, usually ad nauseam.

And the thing is, I felt like I had found my tribe when I landed in that August 2006 chat room. Being pregnant for the first time felt completely foreign. I felt lost and alone, and I was desperate to hear that everything I was experiencing was normal and "okay." And being a first-time mom, I also wanted to be sure I was doing everything right.

And so about forty times a day, I logged in to chat with all my new friends about all things pregnancy, to ask questions, and to read and respond to all the questions that others had posted.

Oh, the drama! At least once a day, there was some new crisis to freak out about—whether the baby wasn't moving enough or whether I wasn't exercising enough or if letting the dog sleep in my bed was hurting the baby or what brand of prenatal vitamins I should be taking or whether my ankles were too swollen.

It got even worse once August rolled around and we all finally began giving birth. First there were the labor plans and the childbirth drama and the oh-so-detailed birth stories to share, followed immediately by a million and one new baby fears to worry about. There were extended—and often heated—debates about co-sleeping and breastfeeding and attachment parenting and all the ways we might be causing permanent harm to these children we were now responsible for.

And I took all the advice I was getting as gospel truth. After all, if everyone was saying it, all these things I was hearing had to be true. Right?

One day, my husband, Chuck, who up until that point had been pretty patient with my hormonally charged daily pregnancy and new-mom freak-outs, finally couldn't take it anymore. He exploded.

"Why are you wasting all your time listening to these random women on the internet?" he asked. "Don't you know that they don't know what they're doing any more than you do? People have been having children for thousands of years, since long before BabyFit. We will figure this out!"

And while I wasn't able to admit it right then, at least not to him, I quickly realized he was right. I had gotten myself so worked up about being a first-time mom and was feeling so nervous and insecure in my abilities that I had thrown all my common sense and gut instincts out the window. The responsibility felt so huge and I was so scared that I was willing to believe that other people had the answers to questions I should have been able to figure out myself.

Not long after that blowup, I gave up the online chat room for good and resolved to just start trusting my own instincts and common sense. And you know what? My daughter Maggie is now twelve and doing just fine. Have I made every decision correctly along the way? Absolutely not. I've made a lot of boneheaded moves as a parent, and I'm sure I'll continue to mess up on a regular basis. But learning to trust my instincts and start using common sense was definitely the right move. And let me tell you, it's a whole lot less stressful too!

And while that may be an extreme example, I've found that this same type of scenario plays out in life all the time, whether it's at work or at church or even in the news. People love to jump on the bandwagon, and it's easy to get caught up in the momentum of a popular viewpoint and forget that it's always important to pause and ask yourself whether what "everyone" is saying actually rings true.

QUESTION AUTHORITY

Just as we need to dare to trust our own intuition and use common sense when it comes to peer-to-peer interactions and groupthink, we also need to question those rules that come from a position of power or authority.

And that can be hard to do sometimes, especially when for our entire lives we've been told to do the exact opposite. We're told to respect authority and play by the rules and stay in line so we don't get into trouble.

But authority comes from all different places—there is authority in the government and the rules we have to follow in order to be law-abiding citizens. There is authority in our workplace and the rules we have to follow at work. There is authority that comes from God and the rules we follow as part of our faith. There is also the authority that comes from our parents, coaches, mentors, or other people in positions of leadership over us. And most of this authority is legitimate. Not all authority is bad. Not all rules are bad. In fact, without some rules and established norms for acceptable behavior, there would be complete chaos. None of us want to live in a world that looks like some version of *The Walking Dead*.

But not all authority is good either, and few of us ever stop to think about the difference. For the most part, we accept without question the rules handed down by the authority figures in our lives. We may not always like them, but we don't question them.

Following rules is the default option, a part of our natural survival instinct. Questioning our boss or ignoring their rules can get us demoted or fired, so we toe the line. Disobeying the law can get us arrested, so we stay out of trouble.

But what about when authority is wrong? What about when the rule goes against our better judgment or, worse yet, our conscience? Do we dare question then?

A famous experiment was conducted at Yale University in the 1960s to test just that. The researcher, Stanley Milgram, wanted to study the willingness of participants to obey an authority figure who was telling them to do something that conflicted with their personal consciences.

In the experiment, participants were told they were assisting in a memory experiment and that their job was to administer electric shocks of increasing voltage each time the person whose memory they were testing answered incorrectly. In reality, that person was an actor, and there were no actual electric shocks. As the shocks increased, the actor would yell louder and louder until at the very highest voltage, they fell silent, as if they had passed out.

If the participant expressed reluctance to continue administering the shocks, the facilitator told them things like, "Please continue," and "The experiment requires that you continue." What Milgram found was pretty shocking. Sixty-five percent of the participants continued administering the shocks, even when they didn't want to and were clearly uncomfortable doing so.[1]

That study has since been replicated many times in many different ways, and the results have been consistent. As a general rule, two-thirds of participants will continue acting in a way that directly contradicts their conscience or better judgment if directed to do so from someone in a position of authority.

Pretty scary, right? It's even scarier when you discover that the idea for this experiment was inspired by the Holocaust. Milgram couldn't understand why so many people in Nazi Germany had willingly participated in such atrocious acts. But they did.

Authority isn't all bad, but it should never be blindly accepted or simply taken at face value. Ultimately it's our duty to make sure we are at least willing to actively question it, even when doing so feels uncomfortable.

DARE TO BE DIFFERENT

Be honest—how often do you dare to think outside the box? Just because something has always been done a certain way doesn't mean it always needs to be done that way. If you think about it, almost every great invention and technological advancement in our society has happened because someone dared to be different or do something in a completely new way.

But it's hard to be different. None of us want to be seen as strange or weird, or to open ourselves up to criticism or ridicule. And yet, why not? Because when you think about it, what do we really have to lose? Why not push the envelope and see how far we can go? Why not try something new? What's the very worst that can happen, really?

Not long after starting my business, I was invited to join what at the time seemed like a very prestigious collaboration of online business owners that was sponsored by a fairly big company.

Being brand-new to the online business world, I thought I had *made* it, especially when this company decided to roll out a whole new initiative and called me personally to invite me to be part of the beta rollout, which was sort of like the *super*-elite group within this elite group. From what I understood, as part of this new initiative, they were going to promote me and my business like crazy, and I was going to make what seemed like a *lot* of money. I was practically beside myself.

But there was a hitch.

You see, there was a small clique of four women in this group who wielded a lot of power. Their businesses were well-established and well-known, and if it had been middle school (and believe me, sometimes it felt like it), those women would have been the popular girls, the girls that every other girl wanted to be.

Unfortunately, from the moment we met (during what turned out to be a painfully awkward sushi dinner), these four women just did not like me. I don't know why. Maybe they thought I didn't deserve to be there. My brand-new business was nothing compared to theirs. Maybe they thought I was too tall. Maybe they were just mean girls. Maybe it's because I've never been in the "in crowd." All these years later, I still have no idea.

But they were powerful, or at least it seemed that way at the time, and this group of four convinced the company to hire them as consultants to run this new initiative.

The very first thing they did was un-invite me.

I was devastated.

I felt like my life was over. This had seemed like my hot ticket to success, and just like that, it was gone.

But once again it was my husband who helped me come to my senses.

"Why do you even care what those mean girls think of you?" he said. "*Who cares* what everyone else is doing? You are way better off doing your own thing. Just go be *you*."

And once again, he was right.

So, once again, I took his advice. I withdrew from the group and stopped trying to emulate what everyone else in my field was doing, and I started totally doing my own thing.

As a result, my business grew exponentially.

What's more, every person I spoke to who participated in that initiative, the one from which I was disinvited, absolutely hated it. In fact, for many of them, it ended up being a huge, years-long distraction that didn't grow their businesses as promised and made them very little money. While my business was taking off, they were standing still. And many of them even quit altogether.

That could have been me.

Thankfully, instead, it was the moment I realized that not only is it okay to do your own thing, but most of the time, it is much, *much* better.

Because rules are for suckers.

It's not always easy to go against the crowd or use your head and embrace common sense when the rest of the world is being driven by emotion and fear. It takes real courage to question authority and to step outside the box when everyone else is telling you to stay in.

But their rules don't have to be your rules. And for that matter, neither do mine!

So dare to forge your own path. Because you should *never* be afraid to think for yourself.

chapter ten

always own it

Because you are in complete control of the choices you make

In the long run, we shape our lives and we shape ourselves. The process never ends until we die. And the choices we make are ultimately our own responsibility.

Eleanor Roosevelt,
You Learn by Living

In October 2014, Allison Toepperwein found the courage to walk away from a toxic marriage and start over as a single mom. It was painful and scary and hard, and she truly couldn't imagine her year getting any worse.

She was wrong.

Only a few short months later, at just thirty-four years old, she was diagnosed with early-onset Parkinson's, a devastating disease for which there is currently no cure. Now raising her young daughter all on her own, Allison was suddenly faced with the very real prospect that she might not be able to care for her much longer.

She was devastated.

That night, New Year's Eve 2014, she cried herself to sleep, wondering how she would ever be able to carry on.

But when she woke up the next morning, the sun was shining through her window and it was a brand-new year. And in that moment, Allison decided that it didn't matter how devastating the diagnosis was or how bad the prognosis might be. She was going to do everything in her power to fight.

She booked an appointment with one of the top neurologists in the country—a doctor who had done nothing but study Parkinson's disease for the past twenty years. He told her that while there was no cure, the only thing that had been proven to slow the progression of the disease was exercise.

And so Allison started to exercise, even though she had almost no energy. She started by walking the steps of the bleachers at her local high school track, slowly working up the strength to do a little bit more each time. Amazingly enough, the exercise gave her more energy, and she continued pushing herself to do more and more.

Eventually she got into such good shape that she was invited to appear not once, but twice, on *American Ninja Warrior*—the first person with Parkinson's disease ever to do so—and in the process she has inspired thousands of others who are battling the same disease.

It's an amazing story, inspiring in so many ways, but mostly because Allison is an incredible example of someone who refused to let her circumstances dictate what she became. She recognized that while she couldn't control everything, she could control how she moved forward and how she responded to the obstacles in her way. She refused to see herself as a helpless victim of bad luck but instead decided to go all in and play hard with the hand she was dealt.

Allison Toepperwein took complete and total responsibility for her life. It's a lesson we can all stand to learn from. In fact, it's our third principle of courage—**always own it**. In other words: stop playing the victim card.

LET GO OF THE VICTIM CARD

We don't like to think of ourselves as victims. After all, it's a pretty strong word with a lot of negative connotations. Victims are weak. Victims are whiny. Victims are stuck being, well, *victims*.

And yet, so often, we play the victim card *without even realizing it*. Those rationalizations we've made for why we can't be successful, why we can't go after our goals and dreams, or why we can't accomplish the things we really want to do are so close to the surface, such a part of our internal narrative, that they come out before we even realize what we're saying. They are such a part of our story that we don't even recognize we are making excuses.

As part of the research for this book, my team asked survey respondents, "What do you feel gets in the way of achieving your dreams or accomplishing your goals?"

Here's a sampling of some of the most common responses:

- "Feeling guilty for not spending time with my family."
- "Too many other important obligations."
- "Money and opportunity. Timing has to be right."
- "Our family struggles with financial security."
- "I have to work full-time to keep my health insurance coverage."
- "Other family members, friends, society, and my job."
- "Lack of finances and time."
- "My husband puts up hurdles."
- "Lack of energy due to disability."
- "Lack of time. Need more education."
- "Too much bad food in the house, not enough time to exercise."
- "My current family situation, lack of money, and lack of sleep."
- "New and recurring health problems."
- "My husband passed away six months ago. He was

supposed to be part of my goals and dreams. I guess I'm depressed, and I have health issues."

- "Poor self-esteem, a spouse who doesn't support me, too many bills."

More than 10 percent of our respondents cited money or financial issues as the biggest thing holding them back; 10 percent blamed their family or spouses; 10 percent blamed a lack of time; and another 5 percent cited health concerns, being overweight, or a general lack of energy.

On the surface, most of those reasons sound perfectly legitimate. After all, who can blame someone who is dealing with a health concern or disability for not going after their goals? How can someone facing serious financial hardship think about pie-in-the-sky ideals? How can anyone dream big while dealing with major family issues?

Those are *real* problems. *Actual* hardships. *Genuine* obstacles. But a good excuse is still just an excuse.

And as long as you're looking for a reason not to, you'll find one. Excuses come in an unlimited supply for everyone. Yes, some people get dealt a lousy hand. And yes, sometimes life isn't fair. But whining and complaining about it won't change anything, and I guarantee that there are plenty of people out there who have had it worse.

On the flip side, you don't have to look very hard to see that the world is full of inspiring people who defeated the odds and overcame extreme adversity to accomplish incredible things.

Oprah Winfrey was born to a poor, single teenaged mother in rural Mississippi. Abused and neglected as a child, she gave birth at age fourteen, but her baby boy died shortly after he was born. Against all odds, she received a full scholarship to college but then was fired from her first job and told she would never make it as a journalist.

J. K. Rowling was a nearly broke single mom when she wrote her first draft for *Harry Potter and the Philosopher's Stone*, struggling to make ends meet while she also worked to make this big idea come to life. When she finally finished, the book was rejected by publishers twelve times before one finally decided to give it a chance. That book became the bestselling children's book of all time.

Bethany Hamilton was on the fast track to surfing stardom when the unthinkable happened—she lost her arm in a shark attack and nearly died. While most teens would have given up in the face of such an overwhelming injury, Bethany did not. She relearned how to surf, eventually winning several professional championships.

Kris Carr was living the life of her dreams as a young, beautiful, successful marketing executive when she was diagnosed with incurable stage IV cancer and given a death sentence. Instead of quietly accepting her diagnosis, she sought out second, third, and fourth opinions before deciding to radically change her lifestyle, adopt a vegan diet, and seek out holistic treatments. Now, fifteen years later, she feels healthier than ever.

The one thing all these inspiring people have in common is that they refused to let their circumstances dictate who they became. They recognized that while they couldn't control everything, they could control how they moved forward and how they responded to the obstacles in their way.

Nothing they did was miraculous. They didn't possess any superpowers. They were just ordinary people who made the decision to stop playing the victim.

STOP WAITING TO BE RESCUED

We live in a culture that idolizes heroes for their daring rescues and dramatic saves. In fact, the hero idea is so ingrained in our thinking that it is hard to imagine a story without one. Indeed, the hero is the crux of every fairy tale. The damsel in distress has a handsome prince who comes to her aid. Cinderella has her fairy godmother. Even Aladdin has a genie who gives him his three wishes.

Every great story needs a hero. Right?

While this may be the stuff that fairy tales are made of, the need for a hero and the desire to be rescued are ideas that permeate our everyday lives as well. Have you ever found yourself wishing you'd be noticed or, better yet, miraculously plucked out of your current state and dropped into a better one?

Perhaps you've wished your boss would recognize your effort and give you that promotion you've been hoping for. Or maybe that a parent or friend would offer guidance or assistance to get you unstuck, or simply see that you could use a little help along the way. Maybe you're secretly hoping to be discovered for a talent you have yet to share with the world. Maybe you'd just like someone—a therapist, a pastor, a life coach, *anyone*—to show you the way.

Wouldn't it be nice if we could just find *someone* to save us from ourselves?

But here's the problem with waiting to be rescued—life doesn't work that way! Most of the time, the people around us are far too busy trying to keep up with their own busy, chaotic, and frustrating lives to worry about saving you from yours. And ultimately, that makes waiting to be rescued just another excuse! Like playing the victim, telling ourselves we can't do something because we don't have anyone to help us along the way is just one more big fat lie.

You don't need a hero. You are *not* a damsel in distress!

And waiting to be rescued won't get you anywhere. You want that promotion? Do the work to deserve it, and then ask for it. Feeling stuck? Start doing something—anything—differently, and take the necessary steps to get unstuck. Have a talent you want to pursue? Then pursue it. Make a demo tape. Write that book. Get an agent. Go out and get it. Remember, action is the antidote to fear, and at the end of the day, the only thing stopping you is *you*.

Because guess what? You get to be the hero of your story!

TAKE BACK CONTROL

"It's not my fault!"

Let me tell you, if I had a dollar for every time my kids said those four little words, I would be one very rich mama! Because at least once a day—and usually many more—we need to have some sort of discussion about taking responsibility and realizing that actions have consequences, and that while they can't always control what happens to them or what other people do, they can control how they respond.

As a mom, I sometimes feel like a broken record and find myself wondering if they will ever really get it. If you have kids, you can probably relate. But the reality is that taking complete and total ownership for everything that happens in our lives is a pretty tough lesson for all of us.

After all, it's human nature to want to blame other people or our circumstances when things go wrong or when we fall short of our goals and expectations. Our first inclination is to complain about the way we were treated or about all the ways the deck was stacked against us—the unfair treatment, the tragic circumstances, the lack of money—and to make one excuse, justification, and rationalization after another.

It's much easier to point the finger at external circumstances than to acknowledge our own shortcomings. And it's certainly easier to just give up when things get hard, especially when we are handed a perfectly legitimate excuse to not keep going. Who could blame us for wanting to throw in the towel?

But that's exactly why taking responsibility for how you respond to everything that happens to you is such an act of courage. It's putting an end to the excuses and refusing to lay the blame for your circumstances on someone who has hurt you, the terrible things that have happened to you, or whether you've had death or illness or tragedy in your life, had to file for bankruptcy, lost a job, or are permanently disabled.

Not only that, it's making the daily choice to accept responsibility for your decisions without looking for someone or something to blame. It's acknowledging the simple truth that, regardless of your circumstances, you are in control of the way you respond, each and every day.

Remember the concept of locus of control from chapter 6? In his book *Smarter, Faster, Better*, Charles Duhigg talks about the importance of this concept when it comes to getting things done and accomplishing our goals. He explains the difference between having an internal locus of control (believing you are in control of your own choices) and an external locus of control (believing your choices are outside your control), and the impact it has on our lives.

Not surprisingly, people who have an internal locus of control are far more motivated, productive, and successful in life. Becoming more motivated, then, is often just a matter of taking responsibility for your choices. As Duhigg explains, "To teach ourselves to self-motivate more easily, we need to see our choices not just as expressions of control but also as affirmations of our values and goals."[2]

Duhigg goes on to explain how nursing home residents who "rebel" and defy the strict rules and rigid schedules actually do much better both mentally and physically than the compliant residents who just go along with everything. As humans, we are wired to make choices and to exercise control over our surroundings.

And while it may seem scary, this idea of taking complete and total responsibility over your life and your circumstances is incredibly freeing. When you take ownership, you don't have to worry about what happens to you, how other people may treat you, or what obstacles may come your way, because ultimately you are in control.

Oh, don't get me wrong—there will still be obstacles along the way. You'll still face hardships and make mistakes. There will be stumbles and spills, and there will be people who treat you unfairly. But it won't matter, because you are no longer a victim of your circumstances. You are still in complete control of how you choose to respond.

In their book *Extreme Ownership*, ex–Navy Seals Jocko Willink and Leif Babin discuss in detail this concept of accepting full responsibility, particularly its importance in leadership. Drawing from their combat experience, they write:

> As individuals, we often attribute the success of others to luck or circumstances and make excuses for our own failures and the failures of our team. We blame our own poor performance on bad luck, circumstances beyond our control, or poorly performing subordinates—anyone but ourselves. Total responsibility for failure is a difficult thing to accept, and taking ownership when things go wrong requires extraordinary humility and courage. But doing just that is an absolute necessity to learning, growing as a leader, and improving a team's performance.[3]

Indeed, making the decision to always own it, no matter what, and to take full responsibility for whatever life throws your way may just be the most courageous thing you do.

Because make no mistake—it will change everything.

You'll no longer have anyone to blame but yourself. You'll have to let go of your victim card and stop letting excuses stand in your way. You'll have to stop waiting for someone else to show you the way. You'll have to choose to be your own hero. And it won't be easy. But it's incredibly empowering.

Because when you always own it, you will be in complete control of all the choices you make.

chapter eleven

embrace honest feedback

Because everyone needs true accountability

> A body of men, holding themselves accountable to nobody, ought not to be trusted by anybody.
>
> *Thomas Paine,*
> *The Rights of Man*

Not long ago, I stumbled across yet another news story announcing the scandalous divorce of a fairly prominent author and motivational speaker, one who had built a wildly successful career teaching others how to live a good life. While the article was written to shock, it really wasn't all that surprising. After all, it is an all-too-familiar story.

A quick rise to fame and fortune, prestige and power, adulation and adoring fans, followed by a stunning downfall, whether due to drug abuse, marital infidelity, overspending, or just a whole lot of really bad choices. From celebrities to megachurch pastors, politicians to athletes, entrepreneurs to business moguls, there is no shortage of tragic tales.

But if you look closely at most of these stories, no matter how different each of these people may be, you'll find one common denominator across the board: a serious lack of accountability.

Celebrities, politicians, and others with power or money or fame who find themselves spiraling out of control are usually the ones who have surrounded themselves with "yes people"—sycophants and leeches who tell them the things they want to hear but don't really have their best interests in mind. As a result, they become more and more out of touch with reality. They start to believe their own hype.

And bad decisions happen when there's no voice of reason or when the voice of reason is ignored or silenced. Bad decisions happen when there is no counterpoint and no discussion. Bad decisions happen when one person suddenly has free rein to do whatever, whenever. Absolute power corrupts absolutely.

It's like a child who hears nothing but praise and is never told no. It doesn't take long for that child to turn into a spoiled, selfish brat. Everyone needs some sort of accountability.

In 2015, Lara and Roger Griffiths were thrilled to discover they had won a nearly $3 million lottery jackpot.[4] They immediately got busy spending it, first purchasing their dream home and a Porsche and a Lexus SUV and then enrolling their two daughters in a pricey private school. They bought a spa for Lara to run. They went on luxury vacations and collected designer jeans and handbags.

But what they didn't do was sit down together and make sure they were on the same page and that they had some sort of plan for their money. Nor did they seek the advice of reputable advisers. Instead, Roger told Lara he could "handle" the money, and Lara, without any real concept of how much they had, simply spent it.

Within six years, it was all gone. Not only that, they were deeply in debt. Their marriage fell apart. They lost their home, the cars, and everything else.

The Griffiths are definitely not alone. In fact, it is estimated that 70 percent of lottery winners go bankrupt within five years of receiving their giant windfalls, largely because these winners lose touch with reality and start to think they are invincible.[5] And while the best thing to do would be to rely on a third party—a reputable financial adviser or attorney—to help manage their windfall, very few lottery winners do.

As humans, we are fundamentally flawed and predisposed, in the absence of any limitations or boundaries, to make really, really stupid decisions! While it's easy to cast judgment on celebrities who crash and burn, politicians who are brought down by scandal, or lottery winners who go bankrupt, the reality is that none of us are completely immune to the seduction of money, power, glory, and adulation, not to mention the temptation to be lazy, make bad choices, and succumb to our vices.

And that is why we *need* accountability in our lives! We need truth-tellers and naysayers, people who love us enough to call us out when we're going down a bad path and who care enough to get in our face. We need people we can trust enough to give us honest feedback, and people to whom we can give that feedback in return.

It's not always easy to accept things we don't want to hear—the hard truths, constructive criticism, and dissenting points of view. We don't really want to deal with someone telling us we might be making a mistake, looking at a problem from the wrong angle, or forming an opinion based on insufficient information.

That is exactly why true accountability—accepting honest feedback and being willing to follow up on it—is such an act of courage. It means becoming vulnerable and admitting you might not have all the answers. It requires being open to sometimes heated discussion and to ideas that aren't yours. It means acting on wise counsel that may have initially conflicted with your opinions and desires. It demands both humility and trust.

A FOUNDATION OF TRUST

I'm a huge fan of the StrengthsFinder personality assessment. In my company, we require all prospective employees to take it as part of the application process, and we actively work to make sure team members are given the opportunity to work in their strength zones. I'm so obsessed that I also had my kids take the kids' version of the test, and then, after much begging and pleading, I persuaded my husband to take it so we could read the *Strengths Based Marriage* book together.[6]

It came as no surprise to either of us that, with the exception of one strength we share—strategic—his top ten strengths are my bottom ten strengths, and vice versa.

We are as opposite as two opposites can be.

And while we already knew that—it would be hard not to—discovering how our strengths play into our personalities and into our marriage was amazingly insightful. We realized that our biggest recurring fights as a couple can be directly tied to the fact that my bottom strength—adaptability—is his number one strength. And what do we fight most about? The fact that I always want to have a plan, and he never does! We both drive each other crazy!

The thing is, until we made the connection that this particular strength (or lack of it) was an intrinsic part of our respective personalities, we both thought the other one was *trying* to drive us crazy. Chuck would think I was purposely trying to annoy him by constantly needing to make a plan, and I would assume he was just being a jerk by resisting.

As it turns out, neither of us was doing it on purpose! And while I won't say we don't still fight about that topic, our conflict in that area has been greatly reduced. I'm more sensitive to the fact that Chuck just needs to go with the flow, and he realizes that without a plan, I feel completely lost.

Taking the time to learn this about each other helped us build a deeper sense of trust—something that is essential in any relationship. If I didn't trust the fact that my husband loves me unconditionally and that he'll always have my back, no matter what, then it would be easy to assume that anytime he does something I find annoying or questions me or challenges me on an idea, he is doing it out of spite or to push my buttons or because he has some secret sinister motive.

Trust is the foundation of every successful marriage, friendship, or accountability partnership. Without it, there is nothing. An empty shell of superficiality. A transactional association based only on what each party may be able to gain. A mutual exchange of pleasantries and platitudes, but nothing more.

And so, in order to trust, you have to be willing to be vulnerable, to let your guard down, and to let the other person see the real you—the quirky, flawed, messed-up, and less-than-perfect version you normally try to keep hidden. You have to be honest about your thoughts and hopes and dreams, as well as your fears and frustrations and insecurities. What's more, you must be willing to see and accept that side of the other person as well.

My husband sees the worst of me—my bad moods and PMS; my freak-outs when something doesn't go according to plan; my impatience with the kids and him and waiting and, well, almost everything; my sudden-onset, completely irrational crabbiness when I get hungry; my obsessive nature; my tendency to make up silly songs that have no tune; and a million other little things that I would be too embarrassed to share.

And while my husband and I, being as opposite as we are, can certainly drive each other crazy sometimes, we also make each other better. He is the sharpener of my sword, and I of his.

I'm also incredibly fortunate to have a handful of friends who know me almost as well—people who I know have my back, no matter what, and people for whom I would literally walk through fire.

Those are *my people*—the ones I trust to tell me when I'm being an idiot or that my head has gotten too big. The ones who will lovingly tell it to me straight, no matter what. I *need* that perspective to keep me grounded.

We all do.

ENCOURAGING CONFLICT

Once a year, my entire team comes to our company headquarters in Florida for our annual planning meeting and team retreat. It's our time to bond as a team, to work through issues, and to dream about the future. As a mostly online company whose employees work remotely, we've found this face-to-face time to be absolutely priceless.

And truthfully, my team is amazing. I know a lot of people say that, but in this case, it's true. There is not a single person who doesn't give 100 percent every day. They love our company, are inspired by the work we do, and could not be more *all in*. Every day I wake up grateful that I get to work with this particular group of individuals.

Last year, in preparation for our retreat, I asked every member of the team to read Patrick Lencioni's book *The Five Dysfunctions of a Team*.[7] Told in parable format, the book uncovers five group behaviors that will always prevent a team from performing at its best.

I had read the book earlier in the year, and what I read worried me, because up to that point, I hadn't thought of our team as dysfunctional—not even a little bit. We all got along and had fun at work, even as we worked really hard, and every member of our team was so positive *all the time* that it practically bordered on annoying.

But that was exactly the problem.

There was *zero* conflict.

In our company, every new idea and initiative was embraced and cheered. It was all encouragement and positivity and warm fuzzies and "great job!" We were really, really good at being nice, at showing appreciation, at showering each other with praise and compliments, at celebrating birthdays and anniversaries and company wins, and at recognizing a job well done.

And while this may all sound like we have a wonderful place to work—and we do—it was also problematic. You see, in our eagerness to get along and always be positive, no one was fighting for the best ideas or daring to speak up when they noticed something was wrong. Our lack of conflict was making us complacent and was actually making the quality of our work suffer.

As a team, we realized that encouraging constructive conflict and holding each other accountable were two things we really needed to work on, and over the past year, that's exactly what we've done.

Meetings now have a lot more spark to them, as team members are increasingly willing to speak their mind, share their opinions, fight for or against a particular idea, and even call each other out when necessary. There is still *plenty* of positivity, but now we celebrate and cheer for those constructive conflict moments. In fact, when we do all agree—which still happens frequently—we often ask one or two people to play devil's advocate, just so we can create more constructive conflict and be absolutely certain we are considering all sides.

A little conflict and controversy are necessary sometimes, and not just when it comes to teams. My siblings and I recently discovered this as we dealt with issues related to my mom's care and finances. We had some strong differences of opinion over the best course of action, and we needed that constructive conflict to bring us to the best course of action.

And you know what? It was *hard*. Really hard. There were some pretty harsh words exchanged and a lot of hurt feelings. We discovered just how deeply rooted in past hurts our conflicts were, and while I know we all have our mom's best interests at heart, we've struggled to agree on the steps that need to be taken. And while we haven't quite yet sorted through it all, I do have faith that eventually, because we care deeply for my mom and for each other, we will work through the conflict and come out on the other side.

It's important to hear other points of view, even when you don't agree with them. Listening to the thoughts of someone who doesn't agree with you forces you to solidify your own beliefs. And fighting to make things better will get you better results.

So don't fear conflict. Instead, embrace honest feedback. Because everyone needs true accountability.

chapter twelve

there are no mistakes, only lessons

Because every breakdown leads to a breakthrough

I haven't failed. I have just found 10,000 ways that won't work!	*Thomas Edison*

Sometimes I feel like my whole life has been a series of wrong turns.

At seventeen, I dropped out of high school to become an exchange student in the Netherlands because I couldn't stand the thought of living at home one more year. No one from my small-town high school had ever been an exchange student before, and they refused to accept the credits from my Dutch school or issue me a diploma. Despite having never graduated from high school, through some sort of weird oversight, I somehow still got accepted to college. But then I dropped out of college too.

I got married at twenty to a guy I liked but didn't love, and I ended up divorced at twenty-two. And then (as I briefly mentioned earlier) I went completely off the deep end, attempted suicide multiple times, and spent more than two years in and out of psychiatric hospitals. During that time, I completely neglected my finances, which ultimately led to filing for bankruptcy.

Twenty-four and newly single, I fell hard for one guy who strung me along for nine painful months and then rebounded with another who ended up being the slimiest of sleazebags, which I only discovered when he made me leave a restaurant through the back door so he wouldn't get busted when his "real" girlfriend showed up.

At twenty-five, I finally pulled my life together, finished college, and worked my tail off to take the GMAT exam and the LSAT and get accepted to a dual-degree JD/MBA program at Washington University in St. Louis. Then I uprooted my entire life, moved across the country, and bought a house, only to drop out of the program eight months later.

Just shy of thirty, I accepted a job as the director of a failing day spa, one that was literally gushing money and losing $50,000 a month when I took it over, with the delusional idea that I could somehow turn it around. I then spent almost two years pouring every ounce of my blood, sweat, and tears into fixing it, only to have it fail anyway.

By the time I was thirty-three, I was a restless stay-at-home mom spending most of my free time (which was a lot) shopping at Target, so much that my husband and I were constantly fighting about money and my spending habits, and, truth be told, I wasn't quite sure if we were going to make it.

And while, at forty, I'd like to pretend that all those mistakes are far in the past and that since starting my business I've somehow managed to get life all figured out, the truth is that I continue to make boneheaded moves almost every single day. I've invested my time and money into projects that failed. I've trusted the wrong people and made more bad hires than I can count. I've looked for other people to give me the answers or show me the way, only to discover that those people don't have any idea what they're doing either. I've made some really bad calls, decisions that in hindsight I wish I could go back and change.

When I look back, I can see all too clearly that much of my life has been a series of bad moves, wrong turns, and major screwups. And yet, what I've realized along the way is that there are no mistakes, only lessons. Every wrong turn has somehow led me to where I am right now. Every misstep has led to what eventually became the right step. And I have faith that the current rough patches in my life will be the future lessons I'll be eternally grateful for.

Because as it turns out, my year as an exchange student was one of the best years of my entire life. It expanded my worldview, which up to that point had been pretty small. I traveled across Europe, experienced independence, and became fluent in Dutch. And while I never graduated from high school, I was able to test out of four language classes and receive sixteen college credits instead.

My first marriage, while an abject failure, taught me a lot about what marriage *shouldn't* be. In hindsight, I accepted the responsibility for how I had failed myself, my husband, and his family and came to terms with my own lack of humility and the things I would have to do differently in the future. I knew that if I were to ever marry again, it would be for the right reasons, to the right guy, and it would be for life.

Filing for bankruptcy was so humiliating that I vowed I would never again get trapped by a financial situation that left me with so few options. I realized that the way to control my own destiny was to earn enough money to have choices.

My time spent battling depression taught me a lot about people and myself, but most importantly, that no matter how bad things get, there's always a way out, and once you've hit rock bottom, there's no place to go but up.

Even my dating tragedies had a silver lining. Had I not been so distraught over having my heart broken, I never would have fallen for the sleazebag who said all the right things. But had I not met Mr. Sleazy, I never would have met his coworker and roommate,

Chuck, who turned out to be "the one." One dog, two kids, six cross-country moves, fifteen years, and seventeen addresses later, we're still going strong. (And no, they're not still friends!)

Dropping out of law school and giving up the only really *big* goal I'd ever had up to that point was probably the scariest thing I've ever done. It was also the most liberating. It taught me that, no matter what, I always had a choice, which I think was a life lesson I had resisted until that moment. It took me a while to figure out what I really wanted to do with my life, and I was still stuck with $30,000 in student loans to pay off, but I never once regretted walking away from law school.

Running the day spa was a crash course in running a business, and when I look back, I can see that the lessons I learned while in that position have continued to pay dividends again and again in the business I now run. I learned how to lead a large team and how to navigate a variety of personalities and styles. I learned how to manage profits and losses, how to be a better marketer, how to sell, how to network, and what it means to provide exceptional customer service.

My Target habit—and the desperate need to find a new hobby before my spending destroyed my marriage—was ultimately what led me to start writing a blog called *Living Well Spending Less*, a personal passion project that eventually blossomed into a full-fledged business. And every day in that business, I continue to discover that the very best lessons almost always come directly from my biggest mistakes. Learning what not to do and what doesn't work helps me figure out what *does* work.

Because in the end, **there are no mistakes, only lessons**—our next principle of courage.

REFRAME YOUR PERCEPTION

What would it mean in your life to stop being afraid of making a mistake? Have you ever thought about that? What would it look like to reframe every experience you've ever had as a time you learned something instead of as a time you messed up? What if you could actually convince yourself—and really, truly believe in your heart of hearts—that *there is no such thing as a mistake?*

How freeing would that be?

The thing is, in life (and in business), it's easy to wish for a smooth ride. Wouldn't it be nice if things always went our way? If we always got everything we wanted, if life was nothing but sunshine and roses and unicorns all the time, and if everything we touched turned to gold? I think deep down, we all know that's not the way it works. But here's something we might not realize: wishing for a smooth ride is counterproductive to creating a life we love.

Because those bumps in the road? Those bumps are where we learn all the good stuff! In life and business, I guarantee that you will always learn the most from the mistakes that you make. Within every mistake or misstep is a golden opportunity to grow and get better.

I know it's no fun to make mistakes or to have things go wrong. But you don't want the fear of failure to be what holds you back from going for it or from trying new things. Because as I've said before, mistakes and failures are a different kind of win. And that's great, because it means that even when you lose, you win!

A FATE WORSE THAN FAILURE

It's easy to convince ourselves that making a mistake is the most terrible thing that could ever happen. We avoid taking risks or stepping outside of our comfort zone and don't go after those big goals and dreams because we can't imagine what would be more devastating than failure. We believe screwing up is the worst-case scenario.

But that's not true.

There is a fate worse than failure—far worse. A consequence of not trying that will ultimately haunt us far longer than the repercussions of making a mistake or the fallout from trying and failing.

It's the pain of regret.

When I look at my life so far, despite the many, many mistakes I've made, I don't actually have that many regrets. Don't get me wrong—there are a lot of experiences I wouldn't want to repeat and a lot of mistakes I'm not proud of, but I'm not sorry they happened.

Even financial mistakes—times I've taken a chance and lost money—don't bother me too much. For instance, several years ago, when oil prices were at a historic high, Chuck and I had an opportunity to invest in drilling for a new oil well. It was far from a sure thing, and it meant taking a pretty big risk, but it also offered a pretty big potential return.

We talked about it at length, weighed the pros and cons, and ultimately decided to go for it. We said a little prayer and wrote a big check. Unfortunately the drilling was a bust. We didn't strike oil or natural gas—or anything at all, for that matter, besides a whole lot of rock.

We lost our entire investment. And while that obviously wasn't ideal or the way we had hoped things would turn out, we also discovered it wasn't the end of the world. We survived the blow, and life went on just as before. We never regretted taking the risk.

But there is one chance we didn't take that I wish we would have.

A couple of years ago, Chuck and I found a historic log cabin for sale in rural eastern Tennessee, just a few miles away from my dear friend Edie. It had incredible potential—a thirteen-foot-wide stone fireplace, great bones, and *so much* character. It also needed a ton of work, from a new roof to all new plumbing and electrical, to a new kitchen and bathrooms and a new septic system, just to name a few. The contractor estimated that we were looking at a minimum of $150,000 in repairs right out of the gate.

It wasn't that we didn't have the money to invest. We did. But we worried about resale value and spending more than the property would ultimately ever be worth. And so, although we really, really loved the cabin, we walked away.

Can I just tell you? Four years later, it still pains me!

We still think about it, talk about it, and wonder, "What if?" And every few months I look up the property on Zillow to see if by some chance it's back on the market. So far, no luck. But maybe someday.

After surveying more than four thousand people for this book, the one thing that stood out to me more than anything else is the unrelenting pain of regret. The couple who chose abortion because they were afraid they wouldn't be good parents. The mom who gave up her dream of going back to school. The dad afraid to give up his steady paycheck to go after that dream job. The real estate agent missing out on clients because she was afraid of being too pushy.

There were so many heartbreaking stories!

In fact, after reading story after story of individuals who let fear hold them back, I'm convinced that nothing is quite as devastating as having to live with the long-term consequences of wishing you could go back and try again.

Because while the fear of failure is very real, it's clear that the temporary pain of making a mistake is nothing close to the lingering and haunting feeling that you could have been or done something more.

Mistakes only hurt for a little while, but regret can follow you for the rest of your life.

So don't let it. Let your fear of regret be stronger than your fear of failure. Dare to take those risks so you don't have to spend a lifetime wondering, *What if . . .?* Be okay with making mistakes.

And if there *is* something you regret? Put it in the past and give yourself permission to move on. Focus on the only thing you can control—the choices you make from here on out. And remind yourself: there are no mistakes, only lessons.

Because every breakdown leads to a breakthrough.

chapter thirteen

balance is overrated

Because if everything is important, nothing is

Something is always born of excess: great art was born of great terror, great loneliness, great inhibitions, instabilities, and it always balances them.

Anaïs Nin, The Diary of Anaïs Nin

Every year in my company, I send out an in-depth survey to find out just a little bit more about our readers and customers—asking questions about likes, dislikes, and where we can improve. I usually ask at least a few questions about goals, and for the past couple of years, I've also asked respondents to identify the one word they'd choose as their "word of the year."

Do you know what word consistently comes up, again and again, usually more than any other word?

Balance.

As women, we're practically *desperate* for it, or so it seems.

It's this mythical, magical idea always lurking on the horizon, just out of our reach. We think it's our lack of balance that is keeping us from having the life we want, and we convince ourselves that achieving balance is what will make us happy.

And because we're certain we haven't yet achieved this magical state of balance, we're never quite satisfied with where we're at. It doesn't seem to matter what we're working on or striving toward or what season of life we happen to be in, we're consistently plagued by an underlying feeling that our life is somehow out of whack and off-kilter, a sense that when we spend too much time on any one thing, we are doing something *wrong*.

For those of us with kids or a family, there's even a special name for this feeling.

Mom guilt.

It's that feeling we are doing something wrong or neglecting our family or somehow damaging our children anytime we take care of ourselves, or focus on our career, or pursue one of our own passions or dreams. (And for the record, you don't have to be a mom to experience it!)

It's the guilt we have about saying no or even "not right now"— the guilt we have for not cooking every meal from scratch or for not spending hours scouring Pinterest in order to create clever *bento* box lunches. It's the guilt we feel for putting our kids to bed twenty minutes early so we can watch Netflix in peace or for not chaperoning this month's field trip or heading up the latest committee or fund-raiser.

It's omnipresent guilt, always there in the background. All. The. Time. The little nagging voice that keeps telling us we should be more, do more, love more, nurture more, give more, serve more, be more present, be more spiritual, and be more intentional.

That little voice telling us that whatever we've done, it's probably not enough.

But what if that voice is lying to us?

What if this idea of balance that we've convinced ourselves is not only possible but desirable actually isn't? What if it's just a myth? A fairy tale? A trap designed to hold us back from whole-heartedly pursuing our goals and dreams?

What if *balance* is somehow overrated?

As a working mom with a very busy and oftentimes incredibly demanding job, I certainly struggle with this dilemma on a regular basis—almost every single day, as a matter of fact. How can I be a good mom and a good wife and a good boss all at the same time? How can I focus on growing my business, leading my team, and achieving all those big goals and dreams that well up inside me, without letting down the people around me? After all, it's not just *me* I have to think about. How do I balance my ambition with my responsibilities?

Because the reality is that it takes a lot to make a dream come true. There's a whole lot of hard work and sacrifice involved in pursuing a big goal. It means making difficult choices, and sometimes it means prioritizing one important and worthwhile thing over another worthwhile and important thing. It also requires a willingness to believe in yourself and trust your choices and your priorities, even when no one else does.

And that's really hard sometimes.

Because as excited as we might feel about reaching new milestones or attaining some big goal, the unspoken question that often remains in the back of our heads is this: *Does pursuing my own dreams make me selfish?*

The answer is yes . . . and no.

Sometimes we have to be selfish in order to get stuff done. Often we have to be willing to make sacrifices or forgo one objective in order to pursue another. At times these objectives will be in direct opposition to one another. And sometimes that's okay. In fact, sometimes that's the way it should be.

So when is it okay to push toward our own goals and when should we hold back? When is it okay to be selfish and when are we supposed to be selfless? When are we supposed to go all in and when should we just dip our toes?

IT'S OKAY TO GET OBSESSIVE

In a culture that pays a lot of lip service to striving for balance in all aspects of our life, the idea of *obsession* gets a bad rap. We're taught to believe that it's not healthy to focus too long or too hard on only one thing or to pour all our energy and efforts into a single area of our life. That we shouldn't work *too* much or exercise *too* hard or practice *too* long.

"All things in moderation," we say.

But is that really true?

I don't think so.

Greatness almost always comes from obsession.

The world's best literature and music and art and food, the most successful companies and inventions, the most groundbreaking scientific discoveries, the most incredible athletic achievements, have almost all been a direct result of relentless pursuit. The most successful and celebrated CEOs, artists, scientists, athletes, and entertainers have always been people who are willing to make sacrifices, to forgo balance in favor of focus in one very targeted area.

Over and over, the story is the same. Years of practice. Intense dedication. Personal sacrifice. Relentless pursuit. In fact, I would dare to assert that behind every truly notable achievement is a person who was willing to get obsessive.

And I also would propose that there is more to this than just obsession. For most of these people, their drive hasn't stemmed only from passion or a desire to succeed, but also from a compelling sense of purpose—a need to contribute to the world and do something bigger than themselves. It's a calling.

As a Christian, I believe we are called by God to use our unique gifts and talents and strengths to the best of our ability. I also believe that the big dreams—the ones that spark fear and excitement inside of us—are divinely inspired. And to me, that means if we don't get obsessive about using these gifts, pursuing these big dreams, and living out our calling, we are actually going astray.

We're not called to balance; we're called to purpose.

With that in mind, what do you think would happen if you gave yourself permission to go all in without feeling guilty? What would change if you were able to stop chasing some mythical idea of balance and instead allowed yourself to get obsessive about going after your dreams or pursuing your purpose? What would that mean for your life right now? What would have to change?

NO SEASON LASTS FOREVER

Have you ever noticed that we humans tend to have complete tunnel vision for whatever season of life we happen to be in? It's all we can see, all we can relate to, and all we're interested in. And because that season is so all-encompassing, it often feels like it will last forever.

When I was in my twenties and single, my life revolved around hiking with my dog, hanging out with my friends, and camping or watching football on the weekends. I was completely free to do whatever I wanted whenever I wanted, and it never once occurred to me that it might not always be that way.

As a newly engaged bride-to-be, I lived, slept, and breathed wedding plans. I read nothing but bridal magazines, watched shows like *Say Yes to the Dress*, and spent an endless number of hours planning the perfect day—the dress, the food, the flowers, the cake, the music, the gift registry . . . it was practically a full-time job! And then, in an instant, we said, "I do," and it was all over.

Pregnancy was a whole new season, one filled with anticipation, worry, excitement, fear, and new television shows like *A Baby Story* and *I Didn't Know I Was Pregnant*. I spent my days reading *What to Expect When You're Expecting* from cover to cover, writing and rewriting my birth plan, and discussing every aspect of my pregnancy in the drama-filled BabyFit chat room.

Motherhood soon turned pregnancy into a distant memory, and every season has brought its own set of challenges and obsessions, from the sleep-deprived baby and toddler years, to the adorable little-kid years, to the not-quite-as-adorable (but far more independent) preteen years. I've yet to experience teenagers, but I'm pretty sure that when it happens, that stage will be all-encompassing as well.

As an entrepreneur, I've experienced lots of different seasons as well. There have been seasons of massive hustle as I worked like crazy to gain traction—barely sleeping, working eighty-plus hours a week, and just frantically throwing spaghetti against the wall to see what would stick.

There have been seasons of creativity and reflection in which I focused on writing a book or creating something new. There have been seasons of building and growth in which I've had to learn how to create systems and build a team. There have been seasons of frustration and despair in which it seemed like everything that could go wrong did go wrong.

Seasons come and go—in marriage and in friendship, in work and in play, in every aspect of our lives. There are seasons of hope and seasons of despair. There are seasons of busy and seasons of calm. Times when we feel productive, and other times when we can't seem to get anything done. Moments of great longing, and moments of contentment.

No season, good or bad, lasts forever.

And that's important to know and remember, because it highlights the futility of feeling guilty about a lack of balance when the seasonal nature of our lives means we will always be at least somewhat out of whack, depending on what season we happen to be in. Seasons change, and with them, our perspective of what matters most.

IF EVERYTHING IS IMPORTANT, NOTHING IS

While it's easy in theory to accept this idea of changing seasons, the myopic nature of these seasons means that in practice, one of the biggest daily struggles we face is the idea that everything in our lives needs to be given equal weight and attention and that if we're not completely balanced in all areas of our lives at all times, we are *failing*.

What a horrible *lie* we are telling ourselves!

Because the truth is, if everything is important, nothing is important. If we are always trying to give equal weight to *all the things*, we will never give enough weight to the really *important things*. Not everything can or should be important all the time. It's not possible, and we'll drive ourselves crazy trying to achieve some sort of perfect balance.

It sometimes feels like succeeding in one area means we need to fail in another area, but what we don't realize is that sometimes that's okay. Sometimes we *should* be failing in one area so we can succeed in another. Because the alternative is being perfectly balanced in our mediocrity.

And who wants that, really?

That's where our big goals come in—they tell us what's really important. Those big goals are there to help us prioritize the areas where we most need to spend our time. They are the road map that lets us know where we are going, where we need to focus, and what activities are not worth our time.

It's the "not worth our time" piece that is really important and also sometimes really hard, especially for those of us who feel like we have to do it all. As with anything else in life, figuring out what's not worth our time takes practice. We need to be constantly revisiting our big goals and then breaking those big goals into smaller goals and determining our priorities accordingly.

That means that taking the time to identify your priorities—the things that matter most to you, based on those big goals—is absolutely essential. It's an exercise that should be done frequently and should result in a concrete list of the things that matter most to you—something you keep close at hand so you can refer back to it whenever life starts to get a little hectic. That list is your physical reminder that not everything is equally important.

Nobody can do it all, and the ones who pretend they can are probably lying. There simply aren't enough hours in the day. We all get the same twenty-four hours, which means that *no matter what we do in life*, we will be faced with choices.

So how do we make sure we choose the right path? How do we know our priorities are in order? Ultimately I think we are all works in progress, subject to continual reassessment and self-reflection, but there are a few principles that have really helped me along the way. They just might help you too.

Be clear about your *why*. It always comes down to this, doesn't it? It's not enough to set big goals; we have to know *why* they're important to us. Because truthfully? If you don't know your *why*, your reason may not justify the sacrifices you need to make to get there.

What is your purpose? What's driving your passion? Is this pursuit something you've been called to? Is it worth making sacrifices for? We'll talk more about finding your *why* in chapter 16, but it's worth raising the question now.

Consult with your spouse, children, or partner. This can be so hard, and yet it is essential to have open dialogue with the people you are feeling guilty about neglecting.

I'm the kind of person who loves being in charge and bossing people around. My husband, by contrast, has no desire to tell people what to do, and he never has. Even so, in all our years of marriage, I've realized that while his gift may not be leadership, it is most definitely wisdom. I have learned and am *still* learning that he has a lot of valuable insight when it comes to helping me achieve my dreams and aspirations. No one knows every part of me as well as he does, and no one will cheer me on as loudly or want me to succeed as genuinely as he does either. What's more, my husband is also the only person who intimately understands the specific needs of our family and who cares as deeply for our children as I do.

Nothing is more valuable than true accountability, and the people closest to you may just be the only people on earth who will be totally honest—at times brutally so—about whether or not you are on the right path. For the sake of your marriage and your family, you owe it to them to listen.

Redeem your time. Because pursuing a dream may require taking more time away from your family than you'd like, it's vitally important to make sure that the time you do spend together really counts. Give your spouse and children the gift of fully engaging whenever you are together. Turn off your phone or computer or whatever other distraction has captured your focus, and give them all of you. Be intentional about setting aside time that is just for them.

At the same time, be wary of giving in to the mom guilt that sometimes tempts us to want to be overly permissive or to give our kids a bunch of stuff they don't need to make up for the times we're not there. More stuff doesn't make up for less time, and trying to be our child's friend instead of their parent won't work either.

Research has shown that after the age of three, it's the quality of time spent with our kids, not the quantity, that matters most.[8] So make it count.

Stop comparing. It's easy to look at our friends and think their lives are somehow better or more worthwhile. We watch our career-minded friends rush off to work each day, looking stylish and put together in their tailored suits and high heels. While they move right on up the corporate ladder, we're still wearing yesterday's Cheerio-encrusted yoga pants. They, in stark contrast, would give anything to be able to stay at home with their little ones, and they worry constantly that they're missing out on the most important things in life.

Comparing your situation to someone else's situation serves no purpose except to make you crazy with self-doubt, so just don't do it. Your path is your path and no one else's.

Own your choices. Every action has its own set of consequences, and every time we select one thing, it means we are *not* choosing something else. So own it. If in your heart of hearts you believe you've been called to a certain path, don't waste time regretting the things you can't do. Understand that when you make a choice to pursue a dream, you are also making the decision to leave something else behind.

And that's okay.

Because none of us can do it all, but we *can* make peace with the choices we've made. And in the end, that needs to be good enough.

And believe this: balance is overrated. Because if everything is important, nothing is.

chapter fourteen

just keep going

Because nothing will ever take the place of persistence

Nothing in the world can take the place of persistence. Talent will not; nothing is more common than unsuccessful men with talent. Genius will not; unrewarded genius is almost a proverb. Education will not; the world is full of educated derelicts. Persistence and determination alone are omnipotent.

Calvin Coolidge

At twenty-three, I was pretty sure I had ruined my life forever. By that point, I had been deeply depressed for more than two years. And I'm not talking about a popping-a-few-Prozac-while-watching-*Steel-Magnolias*-and-feeling-kind-of-glum kind of depressed. I'm talking straight-off-the-deep-end, Sylvia-Plath-style basket case.

My official diagnosis was major depression and PTSD.

Unable to cope with memories of being sexually abused as a child and unwilling to face the fact that I had married the wrong guy and was now stuck in a life I didn't want, I decided that life had no meaning, that there was no such thing as God, and that killing myself was the solution to my problems.

After a couple of false starts, my third suicide attempt nearly succeeded. The firemen broke down my door to get to me, and my heart stopped in the ambulance. They shoved a tube down my throat to keep me breathing, then called my family and told them to come and say goodbye.

But I didn't die.

Instead, I was sent to a psychiatric hospital, where I spent an endless number of hours in group therapy and individual therapy and anger therapy and cognitive behavioral therapy and let's-talk-more-about-your-trauma therapy. In my downtime, I read existential philosophy and bonded with the other patients, who taught me essential life skills such as how to tongue your meds, where to hide contraband, and how to work the "safety" cigarette lighter in the smoke room, which really just taught me it was far easier to simply practice chain-smoking.

Out of the hospital, I headed even farther down my spiral of self-destruction. I started cutting, and when that didn't feel painful enough, I switched to burning. I cut off all my hair, got my nose and my eyebrow pierced, and got multiple tattoos. Still not satisfied, I purposely put myself in riskier and riskier situations—binge drinking, experimenting with sex and drugs, smoking at least two packs of cigarettes a day, and getting into bar fights. I wrote a bad check to buy myself a tent and camped my way down the West Coast until I ended up in middle-of-nowhere Arizona, living with an extremely volatile lesbian couple.

I was a *mess*.

I couldn't bring myself to care. Not about that or about anything else. All I wanted was not to feel, and I did anything and everything that enabled me to avoid the pain I was feeling inside.

Needless to say, the self-destruction didn't help make things better, and after yet another suicide attempt, I ended up back in the mental ward. The doctors gave up on antidepressants and instead turned to electroshock therapy. And then they finally gave up on me altogether and sent me home to die.

And that is how at twenty-three, I found myself divorced, bankrupt, and at rock bottom.

I had no job, no money, no degree, and no hope. I looked like hell—my arms and legs were full of scars from all the cutting and burning—and by that point, I had pretty much alienated everyone who had ever cared about me. Depressed people are not the easiest people to be around, and while most of my friends and family tried to be supportive, after a while, most of them gave up.

I can't really say I blame them. I had given up on myself too.

I went to live with my dad, not because he wanted me to, but because I literally had no other place to go. And for months, I just lay in bed all day, until he finally couldn't take it anymore. He convinced me—bribed me actually—to start working out a few times a week, which I did in the most halfhearted way imaginable. I walked on the treadmill for thirty minutes and then went straight back to bed.

But it did help. Those thirty minutes of literally putting one foot in front of the other eventually started to make a small difference. And those dark clouds of depression that had been hanging over me for so long began to lift, ever so slightly.

I found a new therapist and told her, "I've just spent two and a half years talking about every bad thing that has ever happened to me, and I don't want to talk about it anymore. It hasn't helped, and now I just need to know how to live again."

And for the next two years, that's exactly what she helped me do. Put one foot in front of the other and pull my life back together. I got an apartment and a part-time job, and then an even better full-time job. I adopted a dog, a completely spastic chocolate Lab named Lita that was so full of energy I was forced to get outside and take several long walks a day. I started making new friends—non-self-destructive friends who were actually contributing members of society—and I started repairing the old relationships I had destroyed. I relished being single, had fun camping and hiking on the weekends, and started meeting new guys and going on dates. I went back to college to finish my degree, and I started applying to law school.

My therapist helped me see that every small bit of progress was helping lead to the next one, and she helped me recognize that I didn't have to have my whole life figured out all at once. *I just had to keep going.* And eventually she helped me realize that if I could make it through to the other side of a massive two-year mental breakdown, I could probably make it through anything.

I just had to keep going.

Because there was never a moment in which my life magically turned perfect, and my breakdown certainly wouldn't be the last time I struggled in life. I *did* go to law school, only to realize eight months into it that law school was not for me. I tried many other paths after that, and it would take me years to find my way back to God and to discover the path I was meant to be on.

Along the way, I've faced plenty of challenges and adversity. I've known heartbreak and betrayal, setbacks and failures, crushing losses and bitter disappointments, health issues and money problems, fractured friendships and family drama.

But that's *life.*

No one gets a free pass. None of us are guaranteed a perfectly pleasant journey free of hardship, struggle, and pain. While my story is more traumatic than some, it is far less traumatic than others. There are plenty of people who have experienced far worse challenges, far bigger obstacles, and far more dire circumstances. And the only thing I really know for sure is that there are certain to be more obstacles, struggles, and setbacks in my future—and in yours.

Adversity is a part of life.

The only question is, What are you going to do about it?

THE ONE THING YOU CAN CONTROL

Weekday mornings here in the Soukup household are not a pretty sight.

No matter how early we set the alarm or how much prep work we try to do the night before—packing lunches, signing off on homework, setting out clothes, and putting backpacks and instruments next to the front door—those thirty minutes between 7:30 and 8:00 a.m. always seem to devolve into chaos, yelling, and tears.

The source of all this chaos is no mystery. It is my younger daughter, Annie. The child has no sense of urgency and seemingly no ability to speed up and move faster. She takes forty-five minutes to eat an egg and toast, wears clothes that don't match (which is no small feat, considering the fact that they *wear uniforms*), refuses to brush her hair or tuck in her shirt, and then wanders around holding a shoe, hoping no one will notice she's supposed to be cleaning her room while her sister gets stuck doing all the *actual* work.

What's even more infuriating is that she is seemingly impervious to any amount of yelling, pleading, cajoling, or threat of punishment. She's not worried about being late and is not one bit fazed by the frustration and anger that inevitably surround her. She just doesn't care. Confidence is her top strength, and criticism rolls off her like water off a duck's back. It would probably be an amazing sight to behold if it weren't so darn aggravating.

Not surprisingly, the bulk of the frustration and anger comes from my older daughter, Maggie, who is the person most directly impacted by her sister's behavior. Maggie likes to get to school early so she can see her friends, and in typical oldest child fashion, she is responsible and organized and almost always on time. She's usually ready by 7:30, which means she then spends the rest of the morning trying to get Annie to speed up.

It's roughly the same scene that plays out every morning, our own personal version of *Groundhog Day*. Annie won't get her butt in gear. Maggie gets more and more irritated. There's yelling and screaming and crying and slamming of doors. And usually *a lot* of push-ups, our punishment of choice. (I'm not even joking when I tell you the girl is now so buff that she can drop and give me thirty like it's nothing!)

More than once, Maggie has come to me in tears, frustrated to a level that only a sister conflict can reach.

"Why does Annie have to be *so* annoying? She never does anything! We're going to be late *again*! Why do I have to suffer because of her? It's not *fair*!"

And the thing is—Maggie is absolutely right. It's not fair at all.

Annie has many, many good qualities, but her ability to get herself moving in the morning is not one of them, at least not right now, and most mornings she is 100 percent to blame. As a parent, I'm still holding out hope that this is a phase she'll someday grow out of, but for now, this is our reality.

Because, as I have to explain to Maggie on a regular basis, life isn't always fair.

"Honey, the only thing you can control is *you*. I know it's not fair, but that's just what happens sometimes. And while you can't choose how your sister acts, you can choose how you respond. If you let this ruin your day, you will only be hurting yourself, not her. You have to choose to move past it."

It's a tough pill to swallow when you're twelve.

And it's a lesson that's just as hard for adults.

The reality is that bad stuff is going to happen to you at some point, sometimes through no fault of your own. There are going to be people who treat you badly or who take advantage of you. There will be lots of sucky things in life that you can't do anything about.

And at the end of the day, the only thing you can control is the way you respond. Will you let it ruin your day, or your week, or your life? Or will you choose to move on?

Bitterness, anger, and resentment don't serve you; they only eat you alive. It's drinking a vial of poison but expecting the other person to die. And here's a spoiler alert—they won't!

So choose to accept responsibility for the one thing you can control—yourself. Because even in the worst of circumstances, you still have a choice. Refuse to let the actions and attitudes of others affect the way you act or feel. Refuse to give up the power of choosing how you respond. You can still choose joy and happiness and forgiveness. You can still choose to move on.

And no one can take that away unless you let them.

THE JOY IS IN THE STRUGGLE

So often we're completely blindsided when something unexpected gets us off track. And then, because we're caught so off guard, we are easily devastated and discouraged. We don't know how to handle the obstacle or roadblock that confronts us because we haven't mentally prepared for it.

But I can tell you beyond a shadow of a doubt that the only sure thing in life is that things *will* go wrong.

We've all heard of Murphy's Law—the idea that "anything that can go wrong will go wrong"—but for some reason, we're still upset or surprised or bewildered or angry when things don't turn out exactly the way we expected them to or when we make a mistake or encounter some major roadblock.

We think, *That's not supposed to happen!* and we feel sorry for ourselves, sometimes even throwing ourselves a big fat pity party.

But why are we so surprised?

Bad things will happen. Things will go wrong. Mistakes will be made, over and over again. People will be jerks sometimes. Accidents and tragedies will come out of nowhere. Roadblocks and obstacles will pop up. And the only way we can stop being a victim of our circumstances and a casualty of the things that go wrong—because they *will* go wrong—is to *stop expecting everything to go right.*

We need to stop telling ourselves that the smooth road is the one we are supposed to be on, and we need to stop feeling sorry for ourselves that the road we ended up on isn't the smooth one, because the reality is that *the smooth road doesn't exist.*

Pain and suffering are never fun. No one wishes for hardship or struggle, or for life to be just a little more difficult. We don't relish adversity or things going wrong. We're not secretly hoping for a little tragedy or heartbreak. We don't really want to feel sad or angry or discouraged or outraged.

And yet, most of us, when we look back at the happiest moments of our lives, will almost certainly find they were inevitably tied to some sort of struggle. The things we are proudest of are the things we've had to fight for!

The thrill of completing a marathon is tied to the pain of running for twenty-six miles, and the months of exhausting training that went into preparing for that one moment of joy—all the blisters, sore muscles, and Saturday mornings spent running instead of lounging in bed.

The pride of completing a degree is tied to the years of study—all the sleepless nights spent studying for finals, all the struggling to understand important concepts, and all the investment of time and money.

The satisfaction of owning a successful business is tied to the blood, sweat, and tears that undoubtedly went in to making it work—the stress of endless hours and the feeling of never being done, the anguish of needing to take big risks and dealing with the unknown.

The joy of having children is tied to the exhaustion of raising them—the sleepless nights spent caring for an infant, the temper-tantrum-filled toddler years, the hormone-filled teenage years, and the endless carpools and lunches and laundry and homework and headaches in between.

Struggle and pain and adversity aren't fun, but they do make us better. It's where we learn how to be stronger and wiser and humbler and more patient and empathetic. It's where all the good stuff happens, even if it doesn't feel that way at the time. Within every breakdown is an opportunity for a breakthrough, and even if we don't know exactly what will go wrong or exactly which obstacles will pop up, we can be confident in knowing that *something* won't go exactly as planned. As long as we accept these bumps along the way as an essential part of the process, they are a whole lot easier to bear.

We can keep our perspective through the storm and come out on the other side.

TAKE ONE STEP, AND THEN ANOTHER

In her book *Grit*, research psychologist Angela Duckworth describes in compelling detail how grit—the combination of passion and perseverance—is far more important than raw talent when it comes to creating success in life.[9] She explains that high achievers are not necessarily the most talented, but the ones willing to work the hardest.

We may think we're at a disadvantage because we haven't had access to the same opportunities as someone else or because we've had more hardship or adversity along the way. We may think we're not as smart or as talented or as well-connected as the people we see around us. But at the end of the day, none of those things matter as much as our willingness to just keep going. To take one step, and then another, and then another, and to never, ever quit.

I think sometimes we look at the world as either-or. Either we're smart or we're not. Either we're capable or we're not. Either we're brave or we're not. It's what psychologist Carol Dweck refers to as a fixed mind-set—a belief that our qualities are carved in stone.[10]

And when we look at the world from this fixed mind-set, there's no reason to try any harder. Making a bigger effort is only an opportunity to prove you're not capable.

But as it turns out, our qualities are *not* carved in stone. Courage is never a one-and-done kind of thing. Because it's *never* about how smart or talented you are, or how amazing and original your idea might be, or what degree you've earned or how much money you're starting with. Instead, it's your grit and perseverance and your willingness to work hard and keep working hard that will make all the difference.

You don't need to know every step along the way before you

begin; you just need to take the next one, and then the next one after that. Remember, action is the antidote to fear, which means that as long as you keep moving in the right direction, as long as you keep taking action toward the goal you want to reach (even if that goal is just identifying a goal!), you will get there someday.

Courage, then, is a muscle that needs to be strengthened each day. Courage is a daily decision. It's a conscious choice to take that next step, and then to take the next one after that.

It's the decision to just keep going, no matter what.

Because *nothing* will ever take the place of persistence.

the principles of courage at a glance

1. DARE TO THINK BIG
Never doubt what you are capable of, and know that big goals are the secret to getting and staying motivated.

2. RULES ARE FOR SUCKERS
Never take anything at face value; dare to think for yourself, and be willing to trust your own judgment.

3. ALWAYS OWN IT
You always have a choice in how you respond, so take full responsibility for your response to everything that happens to you.

4. EMBRACE HONEST FEEDBACK
Everyone needs accountability. Surround yourself with people who will speak truth and make you better, even when that truth is sometimes hard to hear.

5. THERE ARE NO MISTAKES, ONLY LESSONS
Don't be afraid to fail, because it's always our biggest breakdowns that lead to our biggest breakthroughs. Live your life with no regrets.

6. BALANCE IS OVERRATED

Stop believing you need to achieve some mythical level of perfect balance in all areas of your life, and give yourself the freedom to go all in with the things that matter most.

7. JUST KEEP GOING

Nothing in the world will ever take the place of persistence. You can do pretty much anything you set your mind to, as long as you refuse to quit.

PART THREE

courage
in action

After adopting a new set of principles—the Principles of Courage—and working to change your mind-set, you're ready to act on those principles and apply them to your daily life. The only way to truly face your fears, overcome adversity, and create a life you love is to take that next step.

Action is the only antidote to fear.

chapter fifteen

claim your target

If you aim at nothing, you'll hit it every time

If you get clear on the what, the how will be taken care of.	*Jack Canfield,* *The Success Principles*

Imagine the following scenario.

You're in an airplane, all buckled up and ready for takeoff. Your bag is stowed securely under the seat in front of you; your tray table is locked; your seat is in the upright position. You even took the time to watch the life-jacket demonstration and read the safety instruction card. You have done your part. You are good to go.

And then, as you're about to take off, the pilot makes a startling announcement.

"Good morning, folks. Thanks for joining us today. We're going to be in the air shortly, but to be honest, we're not really sure where we want to go. We've decided we'll just take off and try to figure it out in the air."

It's hard to imagine, isn't it?

Because obviously a situation like that would never happen

in real life. Every time you get on an airplane, you know where you're going, and, more importantly, so does the pilot. And even if the pilot has to make a few tweaks and adjustments along the way, depending on the weather and jet streams, the general direction is clear. The pilot's job is to navigate the route and make the best possible decisions along the way.

And while it's easy to laugh at the absurdity and complete futility of getting on an airplane without a destination, the reality is that this is the approach most of us take toward life in general a lot of the time. We're just going through the motions, trying to figure it out as we go along, to take care of all our daily responsibilities, and to keep the plane in the air. But without a clear sense of where we're headed, it's impossible to make the best decisions along the way.

Without a target, we will always be a little lost.

And that's exactly why goal setting—especially learning how to think big and setting stretch goals—is so important. We need big goals to actually get big things done and to let us know where we're headed. Without them, we just fly around in circles.

In chapter 8, we talked a lot about thinking big and why it's so important to set stretch goals that will push you past your comfort zone and ignite that fire in your belly. We talked about daring to believe you are capable of more, daring to push yourself past your current limits to create something amazing, and daring to set goals so big that they make your chest tighten or your stomach flutter.

Because *those* are the goals that will motivate you.

Remember, when we set goals that feel safe and achievable, we are caving in to our own preconceived notions of what we're capable of and settling for the status quo. There is nothing inherently motivating about that. Because the goals are comfortable and familiar, they don't require us to stretch or change or work any harder than we already are. And that's when we get bored and lose focus.

But the opposite of that is learning how to claim our target. It's setting—and committing to—a big goal, one so big that it freaks us out a little. And by doing that, we force ourselves out of our comfort zone and into the unknown.

Don't forget—the flutter in your stomach and the tightening in your chest are indications of the good kind of fear, the self-preservation kind of fear that kicks in when you need to do things you don't think you can do. And that's the feeling you want to create by committing to stretch goals.

So let's talk about the three steps for making stretch goals a reality in your life.

STEP 1: DREAM BIG

What would you do if nothing stood in your way? Money, family, education, job—what if none of those were a factor? What if it was just you in a room full of infinite possibility and zero limitations? What would you do? Have you ever given yourself permission to just *dream*, without immediately self-editing or mentally listing all the reasons the idea would be completely impossible?

Most of the time, we're so caught up in the experience of our current reality that we have a hard time imagining anything different. We're so bogged down with all the responsibilities, limitations, frustrations, and obstacles we're facing right now that we can't allow ourselves to imagine, even for just a few minutes, that things could possibly be different. In our mind, our current reality is our only reality.

I can't tell you how often I receive emails and letters from moms who tell me that they want to create big goals but they've been so busy living life and raising kids and taking care of everyone else that they have no idea what their big goals should be. They want to dream big, but they don't know how.

And they're worried that it's too late.

But I can guarantee you that wherever you are right in this moment, you are *not* too late.

Don't believe me?

There are countless stories of famous and successful people who got started later in life.

Martha Stewart published her first book at age forty-one, and she launched what would become a billion-dollar empire—Martha Stewart Living—at forty-seven. Joy Behar was a high school English teacher who broke into show business in her forties. Vera Wang discovered her true calling as a wedding dress designer when she was planning her own wedding at age forty. Julia Child found fame as the first celebrity chef in her fifties. And Laura Ingalls Wilder published her first book at age sixty-five.

And it's not just famous people who have proven that it's never too late to begin. In fact, as part of our research study, we uncovered countless stories of women who, later in life, finally worked up the courage to pursue their dreams or try something new, even as they worried about what others might think or say or that they had missed the boat.

For instance, Cheri Montgomery decided at age fifty-four to pursue her dream of becoming a nurse. A single mom of three teenaged boys, she attended nursing school at night while working full-time during the day, and she ended up graduating with honors at the top of her class.

Marie Bostwick devoted four years to writing her first novel, only to shove the manuscript in her drawer and pretend it never happened, terrified of being rejected. Finally, with her fortieth birthday on the horizon, she worked up the courage to start sending it out to literary agents. And even though it was in fact rejected many times, she kept trying, motivated by the encouraging feedback she received, until she finally found an agent who clicked. Fourteen years and many novels later, she loves impacting the world through her writing.

Amy Love wanted to lose weight and get in shape, but having never been the athletic type, she was worried that she didn't "belong" at the gym. It took her weeks to build up the courage to schedule a consultation with a trainer, but she finally did and then began working out regularly, even when she wanted nothing more than to run away. A year later, she's in the best shape of her life and has more energy and confidence than ever before.

I could go on and on, but the truth is that the only limit on what you are capable of, no matter where you're at in life right now, is your willingness to dream bigger. And that's why it's so essential to give yourself permission to start thinking big without any judgment or self-editing. Let yourself be free to dream about the *what* without worrying just yet about the *how*.

In chapter 8, I shared a list of questions I wanted you to start thinking about.

- What have I always wanted to do?
- What am I interested in or passionate about that I've never dared to pursue?
- What would I do if nothing stood in my way?
- What motivates me or gets me excited to jump out of bed in the morning?
- What did I dream about doing before life got in the way?
- Where would I like to see myself five years or ten years from now?
- What would be the ultimate dream life for me? What does it look like?

Now it's time to get serious about letting yourself dream big. To do this exercise, set a timer for thirty minutes. For that half hour, turn off all those voices in your head that instantly tell you that's not possible, or that's stupid, or who are you to even think about something like that? Just turn them off and dream. Don't hold back. Don't worry about what's possible or impossible. Don't worry about how you'll get there. Don't self-edit. Give yourself thirty minutes to imagine the wildest possibilities, even if they seem completely crazy and unrealistic.

Give yourself permission to think big, and don't keep reading until you've completed this first step.

STEP 2: NARROW YOUR FOCUS

Your next step, once you've dared to start dreaming about all the possibilities, is to *focus*. You want to narrow down your options to the *one* thing you want to make a reality.

You see, in step 1, you had to turn off your self-editing and self-judgment, but this is the step where you can start to bring all those big pie-in-the-sky ideas back down to earth. At least, sort of. Because I still don't want you to rule something out just because it seems impossible or unrealistic or because you have no idea how you'll get there. Don't even worry about that part yet.

But do look at all the things you've dreamed about in step 1, and ask yourself the following questions:

- Why does this idea excite me, or why is this goal important to me?
- Do I feel a flutter in my belly or a tightening in my chest when I think about this goal or idea? Does it scare me? Why or why not?
- On a scale of 1 to 10, with 1 being not that excited and 10 being so excited I can hardly breathe, how excited am I about this goal or idea?

Keep in mind that it's important not to rush this process. Give yourself time to really think about each one of the big dreams or goals you've visualized, to identify your motivation behind each one, and to figure out which one is most important and most exciting to you.

Chances are, as you do this exercise and think through these big goals and ideas that you've dared yourself to dream about, the one thing you are most excited and passionate about will become clear.

When you've asked yourself these questions for every item on your list, it's time to start narrowing down your options. Rule out anything that is not at least an eight on your excitement scale. Don't even consider anything that's not sparking an extreme amount of passion and energy inside you.

And then, from the remaining items, identify the goal or idea that sparks the most passion and excitement—and the most fear—inside you. What's the one that feels distinctly uncomfortable and yet strangely exhilarating, all at the same time? What's the one that feels uniquely purposeful, like it could be a game changer or the thing that finally gets you excited to jump out of bed in the morning? What's the one that feels right?

That's your *one* goal.

And by the way, if none of them make you feel that way, then either you may not be thinking big enough or you're just really out of practice when it comes to setting big goals. In that case, you could do a couple of things.

First, look for inspiration in other places—read biographies of people you admire; try taking a class (either online or in person); consider talking to a trusted friend, a mentor, or even a therapist to work through your mental block. Then go back and repeat the "thinking big" exercise in step 1, and really focus on eliminating any self-editing or judgment.

Next, look at all the things you've written down so far and try ramping them up or multiplying them until they are much bigger and do cause that little flutter in your belly or tightening in your chest and you feel a sparking passion that scares you a little bit. Sometimes you just have to push.

STEP 3: COMMIT

This is where the rubber meets the road. The third step in this process is to fully *commit* to this big goal. Write it down, say it out loud, and do whatever it takes to make it *real*.

This is the truly scary part! This is where your fear—along with your motivation—will kick into overdrive, because you've actually committed to making this big, crazy goal a reality.

It's not enough to dream big—there are lots of dreamers in the world. It's not even enough to pick one goal—there are lots of dreamers with just one dream. The key is in the commitment. You've got to fully commit—both to yourself, internally, and to others, externally—to making this big goal of yours a reality.

It needs to be the first thing you think about when you wake up and the last thing you think about before you go to bed. It needs to be top of mind all the time. It needs to be real. Because it's only when you fully commit that you will be motivated to work a little harder, get up a little earlier or stay up a little later, step outside of your comfort zone, or go that extra mile to do what needs to be done.

What will it take for you to commit to your goal? Do you need to tell someone? Multiple someones? Do you need to post it on Facebook or write it on your bathroom mirror? Do you need to make an investment of time or money? What will make it real for *you*?

Because once you fully commit, you are ready and willing to do whatever it takes for as long as it takes, even when it feels scary and even when it gets hard. It's when you realize that some things are worth fighting for, but first you have to be *all in*.

Yes, you'll probably be scared. Yes, you'll probably feel like you have absolutely no idea what you're doing, at least some of the time. Maybe even all of the time. But as long as you are committed to just keep trying, you will figure it out eventually. There is always a way, even if right now you don't know exactly what that way looks like.

The key to success is grit and determination, and that starts with your complete and total buy-in. You need to commit to your big goal, write it down, say it out loud to anyone who will listen, and make it 100 percent real.

Because once it is real, you can't ignore it, and *that* is where the magic happens. Once you're fully committed to making your big goal a reality, all those sacrifices you have to make—all the blood, sweat, and tears you have to experience—won't feel like a burden or an imposition. You'll do it willingly, knowing that the road won't always be easy, but it will be worth it.

So go ahead. Claim your target. Because if you aim at nothing, you'll hit it every time.

chapter sixteen

find your *why*

Your *why* must be bigger than your fear

If we have our own why in life, we shall get along with almost any how.	*Friedrich Nietzsche, Twilight of the Idols*

In 2014, I founded Elite Blog Academy (EBA) to help teach aspiring entrepreneurs, writers, speakers, artisans, ministers, and activists how to turn their passions into their own successful, profitable online businesses. In the years since, nearly ten thousand students in more than sixty countries worldwide have completed the course.

It's been pretty amazing to watch, but I have to say that one of the very best things about mentoring other entrepreneurs and online business owners is seeing the astonishing transformation that happens when someone takes an idea—often an idea that everyone else thinks is a little bit crazy—and turns it into something real and tangible, whether it's a product or a business or even a ministry or social movement.

There is a moment when people realize that they really can do far more than they ever believed they were capable of, and honestly, I don't think anything is more exciting or more gratifying.

That said, having had a front-row seat to so many of these awe-inspiring transformations, I'm always struck by the one simple thing they all seem to have in common.

They have a *why* that is bigger than themselves.

This was definitely true for Jennifer Marx, a single mom who needed to find a new way to earn a living when it became obvious that the travel guide industry she had worked in for nearly twenty years was quickly becoming obsolete. As her income tanked, she was desperate to find a new way to work from home so she could be there for her daughter, who was going through a rough time.

On the verge of losing her house, and sinking deeper into debt each month, she used her last credit card to purchase the EBA course, and then she put every ounce of effort into completing it and growing her online business. Within a year, she was earning more than $20,000 a month from her site, JenniferMaker.com, and was able to pay off her debt and save her family in the process.

It was true for Caroline Vencil, who believed she had ruined her life when, at just eighteen, she unexpectedly became a teenage mom. Until then, she had always dreamed of becoming a CEO and taking the world by storm. Instead, she got married, dropped out of school, and had two more children in quick succession.

But she saw the potential to start an online business as a chance to redeem herself and create a better life for her family. Just as it was with Jennifer, Caroline's big *why* drove her to put everything she had into completing her coursework. Within months, the revenue from her website, CarolineVencil.com, had surpassed her husband's income, and she had completely changed the trajectory of her family's life—as the CEO of her own successful company.

It was also true for Tasha Agruso, a super-stressed-out corporate lawyer who spent long hours defending doctors in medical malpractice lawsuits and yet who wanted to find a way to stay home with her three-year-old twins—the miracle babies that had taken her more than five years to conceive. The money was good, but the pressure was brutal, and she wanted out.

And so, even though she had almost no spare time in her schedule, she decided to go for it anyway. She spent every spare moment she had working on her home decorating website, Kaleidoscope Living, and within sixteen months, she was making more money through her website than as a partner in her law firm. She gave up her partnership and walked away from the practice of law, and she hasn't looked back since.

In the end, Jennifer, Caroline, and Tasha succeeded in creating successful online businesses because their *why* was bigger than their fear. Yes, they had to work very, very hard. They also had to take risks and try new things, and they had to get up early and stay up late. And I'm sure there were many times when they were frustrated or discouraged or felt like giving up. But it was their *why* that kept them going.

I can relate to all these stories, because when I first started, my *why* was exactly what kept me going as well. I set a goal to make enough money that my husband, Chuck, could quit his job, but the real reason my goal was so important to me was because I knew his job was killing him.

He was *miserable*. And every day, I'd watch him come home a little more defeated, a little more despondent, and a little more beaten than the day before. I knew he felt trapped. We had always agreed that one of us would stay at home with our kids, and as an aerospace engineer, he made a lot more money than I ever believed I could.

It was that *why* that motivated me to learn everything I could about blogging and growing an online business. It was that *why* that drove me to wake up at 3:00 a.m.—and sometimes earlier—every single day for more than three years to work while the kids were asleep so I could still be a mom during the day.

It was that *why* that kept me going, even when it was hard and confusing and frustrating, even when things went wrong. It was that *why* that pushed me to step way outside of my comfort zone to try things that scared me, like making videos, going on TV, attending conferences, and then even *speaking* at conferences.

And it was that *why* that ultimately built my business.

The best way—maybe the only way—to motivate yourself to do hard things, to stretch outside of your comfort zone, and to persevere when the going gets tough is to get crystal clear about your *why*. It won't necessarily make things easier, but it will make the pain worth it. And sometimes that's enough.

Do you know your big *why*? Do you know what's driving you and bringing purpose to your life? Do you know what is worth fighting for? And how can you use that motivation to get you where you want to be?

Find your *why*, and the rest will fall into place.

MANUFACTURE A CATALYST

As part of our study on fear, my research team and I discovered that, without fail, every single story of overcoming adversity or conquering fear included a catalyst for overcoming that fear—some sort of reason *why* that motivated the respondent to take action. Sometimes it was a person who prompted the change, sometimes an event or tragedy, and sometimes just a conscious choice. But there was always *something*.

We were intrigued by this discovery. The realization that every act of courage is preceded by a distinct catalyst prompted us to dig a little deeper to see if there could be a way to categorize these catalysts in a useful way. In the end, we realized that all the different catalysts could be boiled down to five categories:

- trauma, tragedy, or major life event
- an outside opportunity
- accountability or encouragement

- inspiration or education
- dissatisfaction with the status quo and a conscious choice to make a change

For the most part, these catalysts can be spread out on a continuum that ranges from external factors, such as circumstances that are completely outside of one's control, to internal factors, such as intentional choices and circumstances one can control. So, for instance, on the external side of the continuum, an outside catalyst may include a traumatic event or tragedy—something that happened to you that spurred you to take action. On the internal side of the continuum, the catalyst may simply be a conscious choice to act and to not let fear stand in your way.

Where things get really interesting is the range of catalysts that fall somewhere in the middle—those catalysts that are a combination of intentionality and circumstance, of work and luck, of playing the hand you're dealt and letting the chips fall where they may. These include things such as opportunities, which often come from the outside but may also require you to go out and create your own. Middle-range catalysts also include accountability, which can happen both intentionally and inadvertently, as well as inspiration or instruction, which involves both a giver and a receiver.

So why does this matter when it comes to overcoming fear?

Well, it matters because it shows that we have more control than we think we do with regard to manufacturing catalysts that motivate us to push past our fear. Not all of us have the willpower or the drive to just "decide" to overcome our fear—though we are certainly in control of that—but we *can* intentionally seek out inspiration and accountability and better opportunities.

Thus, if you are having trouble connecting with your bigger *why* or finding the motivation to follow through or push past your hesitations, it can be helpful to start by putting some safeguards in place that will keep you connected to that sense of purpose.

If you're trying to work up the courage to start a business, your manufactured catalyst may be as simple as listening to an inspirational or entrepreneurial podcast every morning—something that will keep spurring you to take action. If you're trying to reach a weight-loss goal, your catalyst may be hiring a trainer or joining Weight Watchers to have more accountability. If you're trying to go for a promotion at work, your catalyst may be creating more opportunities by taking the initiative to ask your boss for more responsibility.

If the *why* feels too hard right now, then focus on creating an environment around you that will set you up for success. You may not have control over every circumstance in your life, but you do have control over far more than you realize. Put those safeguards in place and manufacture the catalysts that you know will eventually lead to change.

CONNECT WITH A LARGER PURPOSE

Not long ago, I set a goal to be in the best shape of my life by my fortieth birthday. Having spent eight years focused on growing my business and spending nearly every waking hour in front of a computer screen, I had slowly watched my weight creep up on the scale, assisted by a not-so-healthy diet, in which Doritos was a major food group. I knew something had to give.

It wasn't that I hadn't recognized the problem in the past or even that I hadn't sporadically tried to lose weight. I tried the Cabbage

Soup Diet, the GM Diet, the Fat Flush Diet, the Fast Metabolism Diet, and the Zero Belly Diet, among others. The easy, gimmicky ones usually resulted in a quick weight loss that I inevitably gained back. The other ones were just way too complicated and time-consuming for me to stick with for more than a few days.

And so I started telling myself that growing my business was my priority and that I didn't have time to focus on losing weight, exercising, or trying to eat healthy. I tried desperately to convince myself that the weight gain wasn't that bad and that because I was so tall, it probably wasn't even that noticeable.

But deep down, I was becoming more and more uncomfortable in my own skin. I started to avoid looking in the mirror and began pulling away from my husband, not wanting him to see my body. At work, I stopped putting myself out there as well. I said no to media opportunities and avoided videos and photography. I stopped posting pictures of myself on social media.

I had begun to believe I was never going to be able to lose the weight, and I gave up trying.

But then something happened. I went on a personal retreat and spent five days reading, writing, and reflecting on what was happening in my life and in my business, and what I really wanted. And I had a couple of big epiphanies. The first was that my marriage was not thriving. I was hiding from everyone, including my husband, and we were struggling as a result. Second, my business was not doing well. A large part of our success as a company was a direct result of my ability to connect with people and just be real, and I was no longer doing that.

For the first time ever, I realized that the way I felt about my physical self was directly related to my bigger, far more important— and far more motivating—goals of having a great marriage and a successful business. And as soon as I was able to connect that goal of losing weight and getting in better shape to a higher purpose, I was able to find the motivation to stick with it.

Now, keep in mind that knowing my *why* and connecting to a

higher purpose didn't make losing the weight any easier. I still had to actually do the work of watching my calories and exercising, even when I didn't feel like it. I still had to put safeguards in place, such as hiring a trainer to hold me accountable and signing up for a meal delivery service that made choosing healthy options a whole lot easier. I still had to choose to stop eating Doritos.

And most of the time, it wasn't fun. Because I hate exercise. And I really, really like Doritos. But connecting to that higher purpose did keep me going when things got hard. It reminded me that the sacrifices I was making were worth it and that the pain I was feeling would pay off in the end.

Your own larger purpose might not have anything to do with yourself. Your motivation might be driven by a sense of responsibility or obligation to your family, or to your friends, or to a cause that you believe in deeply. Maybe you feel called by God, and that your purpose is really just to be obedient. Maybe your motivation is wanting to be financially independent so you can finally feel free. Maybe you just want to make a difference in the world.

KEEP YOUR *WHY* TOP OF MIND

Once you've connected to your larger purpose, it's critically important to keep that *why* of yours top of mind and to keep reminding yourself of what matters most, over and over again.

Because it's easy to forget, especially when things get hard.

And make no mistake—things will get hard! Because anytime you're pursuing a big goal or pushing past your comfort zone or facing a fear or about to do something really important or really great, that's exactly when things start to get difficult, awkward, painful, and very, very real.

For me, it wasn't enough to connect to my larger purpose just once; I had to remind myself daily—every single morning—of exactly *why* this goal of losing weight mattered so much to me.

I had to remember how it would impact my marriage, think about all the things I wanted for my business, and remind myself that getting in better shape was the first step on that path. It didn't make me crave Doritos any less, but it did help me stay strong, and it also helped me get back on track those times I did give in to temptation (which is more often than I'd like to admit).

For you, it may mean writing out your *why* in a place where you can refer back to it frequently—in a journal or your planner, or perhaps even on a whiteboard in your office. Maybe you'll need to create an inspiration board—a visual representation of your *why*—or just post a picture that reminds you of your higher purpose. It could be as simple as posting an affirmation on your bathroom mirror—something you read every morning as you brush your teeth.

Or it could be all of the above.

The point is to make sure you're doing everything in your power to continually connect to your *why* and to keep that higher purpose top of mind. It should be something you refer back to daily, even multiple times a day if you have to. It should be the first thing you think about in the morning and the last thing you think about at night.

That way, when the going gets tough, you'll be equipped with a *why* big enough to crush every fear.

chapter seventeen

create your action plan

Break down your big goals into manageable bites

A goal without a plan is just a dream. | *Dave Ramsey*

Not everyone appreciates a good plan as much as I do.

Namely, my husband.

In fact, when it comes to planning ahead, we're as opposite as two people can be. I love knowing what's on the agenda, while he tends to get stressed when there are more than two things on his to-do list.

Thankfully we've learned over the years how to at least tolerate each other's quirks in order to find a balance that works for both of us. I stick to a tight plan Monday through Friday and try to leave Saturday and Sunday open for whatever. I guess you could call it planned spontaneity, or maybe just scheduled free time.

So why am I telling you this? I guess it's mostly to say, before we dive into the nitty-gritty of my own system for planning my time, that I *get* that planning is not for everyone. And that's okay. But I also know that without a solid action plan in place, most people will spin in circles.

In chapter 15, we talked about the importance of claiming your target—allowing yourself the freedom to dream big, but then narrowing your focus and actually *committing* to one big goal, a goal so big it scares you. And I told you to worry about the *what* without worrying yet about the *how*.

That said, there is a point, once you've started to think big and then gotten clear about what you really want and why you want it, when you will need to start thinking about the *how*.

And so while you may prefer to be flexible and adaptable—you may even excel at it—if you want to actually accomplish your big goals and dreams, you're going to need a solid plan. But as we go through this process of creating your action plan, keep in mind that for your own sanity (or your spouse's), you may need to build into your plan some unstructured time as well.

BREAKING BIG INTO BITE-SIZE

So how does it work exactly—this process of taking a big goal and turning it into a plan of action that gets you where you want to be? After all, it's one thing to dream about crazy ideas, but it is a whole other thing to follow through on them. Where does one even begin?

Essentially, creating a plan is a process of breaking down the big goal into bite-size pieces, first from "someday" to this year, then from this year to this month, then from this month to this week, and then from this week to today. It's starting with the big things and distilling them down to the daily decisions and action steps that need to be made in order to get you where you want to go. After all, achieving the biggest goals never happens in one fell swoop. It's always a matter of continual movement in the right direction.

And while this sounds super straightforward—and it is—it's

amazing how many people never take the time to do this. Instead, most people approach their days and weeks with a "what's most urgent?" mentality, focusing their energy and effort on the things that feel important and critical right now without necessarily thinking about how those tasks fit into the larger picture. We're always busy, but not always *purposefully* busy.

The thing about life is that our time will always be filled, and there will always be things to do, no matter what those things are. And for most people, there will always be more things to do than we have hours in the day.

At some point, we have to choose. And if we always choose what is urgent over what is important, the big goals will be impossible to achieve. And chances are good that if you are really struggling with the idea of setting big goals or with the belief that there is just no way to make them happen, you've been stuck in a pattern of choosing the urgent over the important for quite some time.

It's hard to make time for those big goals when they don't feel as pressing as whatever crisis happens to be right in front of us, and when the payout is far into the future rather than right now. That's especially true when a big goal involves something hard or painful or less than pleasant. Our natural inclination is to put it off in favor of whatever feels more important in the moment or whatever is going to give us that immediate sense of satisfaction.

But that's exactly why it is so important to break down the big goals into smaller milestones, and then those milestones into even smaller, more manageable bites, until you've got a set of tasks that feel doable—tasks that, once completed, will give you the short-term satisfaction and sense of accomplishment at checking them off your list, and also the long-term satisfaction of knowing that you are one small step closer to your big goal.

So, for instance, if your big goal is to become 100 percent debt-free, then perhaps one of your big goals this year may be to get all your credit cards paid off, and maybe your big goal this month may be to pay off the credit card with the smallest balance, and your big goal each week may be to review your expenses, and your big goal each day may be to stop eating out for lunch and to stop going to Starbucks.

Likewise, if your big goal is to become a bestselling novelist, then perhaps one of your big goals this year will be to actually write your first book, your big goal this month will be to write the first four chapters, your big goal each week will be to complete each chapter, and your big goal each day will be to write at least a thousand words.

If your big goal is to run a marathon, even though you're currently forty pounds overweight, then perhaps one of your big goals this year will be to run your first 10K. Then maybe your big goal this month will be to run one full mile without stopping, and your big goal each week will be to run at least three times following a Couch-to-10K program. And from there, you will still have to make the daily decision to run or not run.

And by the way, if these seem like big, crazy, audacious goals, it's because they *are*—that's the whole point! If the goals you wrote down aren't big enough to scare you a little bit, then before you move on, you may want to go back and see if you can make them bigger. Remember, the sky's the limit. You'll only achieve greatness if you actually reach for it.

But do you see how this works? We simply take a big goal and break it down into smaller, more doable steps that are easy to stay focused on but will also get you closer to the big goal.

TIME BLOCKING

Of course, where the rubber really meets the road when it comes to accomplishing big goals is when we break down our monthly goals into a list of tasks we can implement each week.

I like to start my weekly plan by using a special planning page I call the Weekly Wizard™, which helps me identify the *one* big thing that is most important this week—the big focus—as well as the top three tasks—the "A" tasks—that absolutely must get done this week to get me closer to my goals.

MY *one* THING

MUST DOS
○ ⎯⎯⎯⎯
○ ⎯⎯⎯⎯
○ ⎯⎯⎯⎯
○ ⎯⎯⎯⎯

SHOULD DOS
○ ⎯⎯⎯⎯
○ ⎯⎯⎯⎯
○ ⎯⎯⎯⎯
○ ⎯⎯⎯⎯

WOULD LIKE TO DOS
○ ⎯⎯⎯⎯
○ ⎯⎯⎯⎯
○ ⎯⎯⎯⎯
○ ⎯⎯⎯⎯

OTHERS NEED FROM ME
○ ⎯⎯⎯⎯
○ ⎯⎯⎯⎯

a *successful* day is

how I'll *celebrate*

MY *focus* BLOCKS
ONE ___ : ___ / ___ : ___

TWO ___ : ___ / ___ : ___

THREE ___ : ___ / ___ : ___

FOUR ___ : ___ / ___ : ___

FIVE ___ : ___ / ___ : ___

SIX ___ : ___ / ___ : ___

THE DAILY FOCUS SHEET © COPYRIGHT 2018

Because none of us live in a vacuum, in addition to our most important tasks, the ones that will get us closer to our goals, there will also always be things in our lives that *should* be done—all those things we used to prioritize because they felt more urgent. And while these tasks are important, they should be considered "B" tasks— items that should be done but not at the expense of our "A" tasks.

Remember, your "A" tasks are the ones that will get you closer to your long-term goals! So while in the moment it may seem more important to respond to an urgent email, tackle that pile of laundry, or get dinner on the table, the reality is that if you want to be more productive and actually reach your goals, you need to focus on your biggest, most important tasks! After all, email will always be there; you can always order takeout; and as long as you still have clean underwear, you're probably good as far as laundry goes.

Then there are your "C" tasks. These are the things you'd like to do if you have extra time but that don't necessarily have to be done and can easily be put off until the following week if necessary. These should *never* be done if your "A" tasks have not first been checked off your list.

As a side note, this Weekly Wizard sheet is available as a sticky note pad, which I then stick right into the weekly planning page of my Living Well Planner®. Both the Weekly Wizard and the Living Well Planner are available online at livingwell.shop.

But once you've filled out your Weekly Wizard, there's one more step to take when it comes to weekly planning. You see, once you have a clear idea of what needs to be done and the order of importance, you'll have to block out time in your schedule to make it happen. Remember, we only do what we make time for, so if you don't block out time for your biggest priorities, the time will simply slip away.

Essentially this is a process of making an appointment with yourself to complete a task and taking the appointment as seriously as you would any other one on your calendar. Start by blocking out the actual appointments—those preexisting events, meetings, and commitments that cannot be moved.

Next—and this is the really important part—block out time in your schedule for all your "A" tasks, the ones that will get you closer to your big goals. Keep in mind that it will feel strange, at least at first, to block out time for things that may not be extremely urgent or pressing right at the moment. But to truly make achieving your big goal a priority in your life, you will need to set aside time and then protect that time the same way you would protect one of the other appointments or meetings.

After you've blocked out time for your "A" tasks, you may want to block out time for your "B" tasks as well, especially the ones that feel most pressing. Again, it may feel strange at first to block out your time so completely, but it's the best way I've found to make sure I can stay on top of all my responsibilities.

Here are a few more tips to keep in mind:

- Always block out more time for an important task than you think you'll need. Things almost always take longer than we think they will! Start by giving yourself twice as much time as you think you'll need, and then maybe drop it down to 50 percent more once you've gotten better at estimating.
- If you can, try to block your time into one- to two-hour chunks. Research shows that this is the optimum amount of time to work in one stretch—long enough that you can really dig in, but not so long that your brain turns off.
- Schedule buffer blocks each day. Buffer blocks are chunks of unstructured time you can use to catch up if you get behind or to handle any urgent matters that come up that day. Keep in mind that the more unpredictable your day, the more buffer time you should include in your schedule.
- Don't forget to account for time spent commuting and/or getting ready.
- Don't be shy about scheduling blocks for fun and recreation— time for exercise, meditation, watching TV, reading, family time, or just unstructured free time. Everyone needs a break

sometimes, and planning for downtime allows you to enjoy it guilt-free, knowing there's nothing else you "should" be doing right then.

The key to success in all of this is to commit to and honor your appointments with yourself in the same way you would honor a commitment to someone else. And like anything else in life, the more you practice it, the easier time blocking will become.

DAILY DECISIONS

I wish I could tell you, now that you've walked yourself through the entire process of turning your big dreams into bite-sized baby steps and learned the secret of blocking out your time, that it's all going to be smooth sailing from here. After all, you've figured out what you want and exactly what needs to happen to get you there. The hard work is done, right?

Not so much.

The reality is that while you've now given yourself a clear road map—or, in modern terms, you've programmed the GPS—you still have to actually drive the car and get yourself to where you want to go.

In other words, you need to make the daily decision to follow through with your plan and actually do the work. You need to make the daily decision to focus on your biggest, most important tasks. You need to make the daily decision to be as productive as possible.

This isn't always a decision that comes easily. Sometimes, especially when it feels hard, we don't really *feel* like doing the work that needs to be done. Other times we're sucked into the tyranny of the urgent—the email that needs our attention, the project at work that needs to be done right away, the snarky comment from our sister, the dramatic brouhaha erupting in the PTA that we swore we wouldn't pay any attention to, the new diet craze that everyone is suddenly swearing by—and it's hard to keep our focus on the big goal.

I read a book a few years ago that forever changed the way I approached my daily task list. It's called *Eat That Frog: 21 Great Ways to Stop Procrastinating and Get More Done in Less Time* by Brian Tracy. The book gets its name from a quote often attributed to Mark Twain: "Eat a live frog every morning and nothing worse will happen to you the rest of the day." Tracy elaborates by writing, "If you have to eat two frogs, eat the ugliest one first."[11]

The point of the quote—and the book—is that if you start your day by tackling your hardest (ugliest) but most important tasks, you will have already done a lot, even if you don't do much of anything else for the rest of the day.

Life moves fast, and it's so easy to get sucked into the mundane—albeit essential—tasks of the everyday. We often spend the bulk of our day putting out fires and reacting to other people rather than proactively working to accomplish the things we really want to do.

The main problem with living our lives this way is that our willpower runs out. Each morning, we start our day filled with a certain amount of self-discipline, and as we go about our day, the resolve tends to drain out. When we start our day by focusing on the mundane and easy stuff, we waste our reserves. Eating our ugly frogs first thing in the morning means having enough energy and discipline to truly get things done.

On any given day, we all have our own frogs to eat. If we're serious about attaining our goals and following through on our dreams—no matter what those dreams may be—then we must make the daily choice to do something, anything, to get us one small step closer to the finish line.

We have to be purposeful about making sure the big stuff gets done first. We must accept the truth that if we don't take the time to put our long-term goals first, *there will never be enough time or energy for our dreams*. The obligations of the everyday will always take over.

Over the years, I've learned time and time again that creating good habits is a key to being able to get things done. The more good habits we can create for ourselves, the more willpower and mental energy we have left over to pursue our dreams.

Thus, if we can make working on our most important tasks a *habit*, something that happens automatically without any thought, the autopilot portion of our brain will kick in and we'll have more discipline stored up to tackle those "B" and "C" tasks too. While it seems almost too good to be true, the fact is that the more we can put on autopilot, the more willpower reserve we will have left for the things that matter. Our daily habits will ultimately determine what we get done, which is why we need to make them count.

That's why I believe that the very best thing you will ever do for your productivity and for your big goals and dreams is to set aside the first fifteen minutes of your day to plan your day.

For my daily planning, I use the Daily Do It™ sticky notes (these can be found online at livingwell.shop). These notes are designed to start your day off right and keep you going strong so you can stay focused on your biggest, most important tasks. The Daily Do It is literally your blueprint to a productive day. It will give you the focus and clarity to actually get things done—often more than you ever thought possible. I know it may seem like a waste of time to go through this process every single day, especially when many of your tasks are the same from day to day, but I promise it will multiply the amount you are able to accomplish.

When we don't take the time to make a plan, we end up spinning. But when we create our own daily action plan and break down our big goals into manageable bites, it's much easier to stay on track.

And that is how our daily decisions lead to big things.

HOW TO USE THE DAILY
DO IT TO PLAN YOUR DAY

MY ONE THING. What's the *one* thing you can do today to make everything else easier? This should be your main focus for the day. Make sure the tasks you choose reflect this focus.

MUST DOS. These are your "A" tasks, the things that will bring you one step closer to your big goals. Put them first on your list so you are sure to make time for them.

SHOULD DOS. These are your "B" tasks, the things that need to be done but don't necessarily relate to your big goals.

WOULD LIKE TO DOS. These are your "C" tasks, the things you would love to get to if you have time but won't feel too bad if you can't. Be careful not to put any "A" tasks here!

OTHERS NEED FROM ME. This is where you include any requests from other people—tasks that you have been asked by someone else to do, but that might not necessarily fit into the rest of your day.

A SUCCESSFUL DAY IS . . . How will you measure the success of your day? What has to happen for you to feel like you crushed it? Is there one thing in particular? Or is it just managing to stay focused all day? Set your intention ahead of time so you have a clear mark for success.

HOW I'LL CELEBRATE. How will you celebrate your win? Celebrating keeps you energized and excited about your productivity and reminds you that you are making progress. Be sure to pick a way to treat yourself!

MY *one* THING

MUST DOS

○
○
○
○
○

SHOULD DOS

○
○
○
○
○

WOULD LIKE TO DOS

○
○
○
○
○

OTHERS NEED FROM ME

○
○

a *successful* day is

how I'll *celebrate*

chapter eighteen

form your own truth club

Surround yourself with people who will make you better

> If you hang out with chickens, you're going to cluck, and if you hang out with eagles, you're going to fly.
>
> *Steve Maraboli*

I always know when I've found someone who is "my people," as I like to say. My closest friends are the ones with whom I can always be brutally real—honest and vulnerable—the ones with whom I never worry whether I'm being judged, and the ones who are never afraid to go deep.

Usually I can tell right away, but not always. With my friend Gry, for instance, the connection was almost instantaneous. We were both attending a small conference, and as soon as she raised her hand and said the exact thing I was thinking—an opinion that wasn't all that popular—I knew she and I were destined to be friends. I ended up extending my trip and crashing in her hotel room just so we could hang out for an extra day.

We had the best time, and then we went our separate ways, and while we texted back and forth a few times, we didn't really talk again until eighteen months later, when I happened to be in New York City, where she lives. I texted to see if she was free for lunch. She was, and lunch turned into coffee, which turned into happy hour, which turned into dinner.

And that's when I really knew. Because the best friends are the ones who will pick up with you like it was yesterday, even after months or years of not talking.

But I love Gry because she will tell me, point-blank, that I am an idiot and that I need to get it together and make a change. She's not afraid to keep it real, and definitely not afraid to say the hard things that other people don't dare tell you. And I like to think I'd do the same for her.

With my friend Susie, the connection wasn't quite as instant. Susie is blond and sweet as sugar, and the perkiest and most positive person I've ever met. She loves nothing better than a party, and I'll admit that when I first met her, I assumed she was an airhead and that we wouldn't have anything in common.

And then we got seated across from one another at a dinner and started talking, somehow, about our childhoods, and about growing up with a mom who was mentally ill. The conversation was deep and raw and vulnerable, and I realized very quickly that I had completely misjudged her.

Because as it turns out, Susie is actually brilliant. Not only that, her perkiness and positivity are not at all superficial but hard-fought and hard-won. Susie has overcome poverty, homelessness, and an abusive first husband—things that would easily defeat most people—and refused to give up or make excuses.

And then there is Laura, who I knew was my people long before I even met her. She was close friends with both Gry and Susie, who both told me I needed to meet her and who both told her the same thing. When we finally connected, it was as though we had been friends forever.

These three women, each smart and funny and real, make up my "Truth Club." They are the ones who will cheer me on and hold me accountable, who aren't afraid to tell me I'm wrong, but who will also let me know when I'm on the right track. They make me laugh. They make me cry. But they always, always, always keep it real. There is no pretense, no posturing, no bull—nothing but truth, vulnerability, authenticity, and a mutual desire to push each other past our fears so we can be our best selves.

We get together in person every few months for three days of masterminding, and we meet via conference call once a month just to check in and hold each other accountable. We text back and forth on a regular basis, sometimes to give encouragement, sometimes to ask advice, but always to offer support.

I couldn't be more grateful for these three women and for the other deep and real friendships I've made throughout the years. I love having people in my life who will tell me the truth, no matter what, and the older I get, the more I realize just how valuable it is to have these types of relationships in my life—friendships that don't just scratch the surface but foster true accountability. Relationships that make you believe you are capable of more.

WHO YOU SURROUND YOURSELF WITH IS WHO YOU BECOME

Author and entrepreneur Jim Rohn once said we are the average of the five people we spend the most time with.[12] And while that may be overstating it just a little, the reality is that our friendships and relationships do have a huge impact on the way we live our lives, whether we realize it or not.

The pressure to fit in and conform starts young and never really goes away. We dress a certain way, talk a certain way, participate in certain activities, watch certain TV shows, eat certain foods, cheer for certain sports teams, like certain celebrities, drive certain

196

vehicles, vote a certain way, shop at certain stores, read certain books, and discuss certain topics because the people around us—the circle we've surrounded ourselves with—are doing the same thing.

We think we're making our own choices, but are we really? How much would our tastes change if we were suddenly uprooted and plunked down in a community completely different from the one we're in right now?

Last year, my husband and I moved our family back to my hometown of Lynden, Washington, for a year so we could be closer to my mom, who had recently been diagnosed with dementia. With a population descended primarily of Dutch immigrants, Lynden is one of those picturesque towns that seems too quaint to be real. Having grown up in that small town, I never really noticed all the subtle social norms and behaviors that are unique to the community, but my husband, an outsider, definitely did.

For instance, in Lynden, whenever you meet someone new, you have to "make the connection." It's a process sometimes called "Dutch Bingo." You find out who the person's family is and figure out how they might be connected to you, whether it's through church, school, or familial ties. Chuck always found it odd that complete strangers would somehow connect that his father-in-law's cousin once removed was married to their great-aunt's sister-in-law (or something like that!).

And there were other things we noticed too as we lived in that small town for a year. Many of the moms had a very distinctive style—similar to one another but very different from the way the moms dressed in Florida. No one mowed the lawn on Sunday. Conversations tended to center around sports. It wasn't that everyone was purposely trying to conform, but there was a very distinct culture, and just by living there, you couldn't help but be impacted by it.

Granted, Lynden is unique in that most people have lived there their whole lives, in families that have been there for generations, which makes it somewhat of a closed society. And while most social circles are not quite *that* homogenous, they do tend to develop their own sets of norms.

And there's nothing necessarily wrong with that, as long as you're sure that the norms you are conforming to—consciously or not—are the norms you actually *want* to be conforming to.

If you work in an organization where people tend to be negative and unmotivated or where the culture includes a lot of complaining and gossip, you will probably at some point find yourself stepping into that mode too. If the women at the gym you go to look more like they're ready for the runway than the treadmill, you may start putting a little more effort into your workout wear too. If everyone at your church speaks in "Christianese," you'll probably start speaking it too—often without even realizing it. If the parents in your circle obsess about getting their kids into the "right" college or on the "right" club soccer team, you probably will too.

And if the people you surround yourself with don't operate with a growth mind-set—if they aren't interested in pushing past their comfort zones or trying new things or setting big goals—then it can be really hard to find the motivation to do that in your own life, at least on an ongoing basis.

So what's the solution? Should you ditch all your friends in favor of better ones? Do you leave your spouse and family members behind? How do you create a new culture of growth around yourself when you still have to live your life in the old culture? How do you break free from the social norms that may be holding you back without burning all your bridges?

It's not as impossible as it may feel.

FINDING YOUR TRIBE

Let me just say for the record that I don't think abandoning your family and ditching all your friends is the right solution. That said, if you've realized that the social norms of your current circle may be holding you back from exploring your full potential or keeping you stuck in a pattern you don't want to be stuck in anymore, then it may be time to expand your circle and perhaps even allocate your time more selectively.

I promise you there *are* people out there in the world who are *your* people—ones with whom you will feel a strong connection, ones with whom you can be real and authentic, ones who will push you to be better and who won't be afraid to hold you accountable when you need it. There are people waiting for someone just like you to brighten and enrich their lives in the same way they will be able to brighten and enrich yours.

But *you* will have to find them.

It will probably mean stepping outside of the comfort zone of the people you already know and associate with in order to make new friends. It may mean reaching out to someone you don't know well but who may be a person you've admired or looked up to from afar. It may mean trying new activities—perhaps taking a class, attending a conference, connecting in a Facebook group or an online forum, joining a book club or the Chamber of Commerce, or even finding a membership community such as Doing It Scared, which you can find at doitscared.com.

I know all of that can feel a little scary at first, especially if you've lived your whole life within the same small circle. But I promise it does get easier with time. And what's more, once you open yourself up to the possibility of meeting and making new friends, you'll be amazed at how the right people start to show up in your life.

It's sort of like when you're thinking about buying a new car—a phase I just happened to be in recently. I did my research, read the reviews, thought a lot about what I wanted, and eventually narrowed my choices down to two—a Ford Explorer and a Lincoln MKC.

Now, before I was thinking about a new vehicle, I never paid attention to cars. Why would I? For five years, Chuck and I shared a car, and he drove me almost everywhere. But then, once it was on my mind, cars were all I would see when I was out and about. And do you know what cars I noticed more than any others? The Ford Explorer and the Lincoln MKC. It felt like they were literally everywhere I went!

Now does that mean there was suddenly a huge influx of Fords and Lincolns on the road? Did the factory have some sort of over-production crisis that happened to coincide with my desire to get a new vehicle?

Of course not.

I saw those particular vehicles everywhere because that's what my brain was tuned in to see. And it's the same way with people. When you identify the type of friendships you are looking for, your brain becomes wired to see those opportunities. Sometimes you just have to start by setting your intention.

HOW TO FOSTER REAL ACCOUNTABILITY

But what do you do once you've found your people? How do you deepen those relationships, create meaningful dialogue, and foster real accountability, the kind we talked about back in chapter 11? How do you actually *form* your own Truth Club?

It starts by finding at least one trustworthy person who can provide the accountability and support you're looking for and who is open to receiving that same sort of accountability and support in return. You may even want to create this sort of relationship with multiple people for different areas of your life. For instance, you may want someone to hold you accountable from a business standpoint, but you may also want accountability for losing weight, being a better parent, or deepening your spiritual life.

For example, in addition to my Truth Club, I have several other close friends who provide accountability in different ways. My friend Bonnie, whom I've known since our kids were in preschool together, meets me regularly for lunch to talk honestly about the challenges of running a business and being a mom. My friend Alysha, who has known me since sixth grade, is always able to bring a broader perspective to problems than anyone else can bring. My friend Edie is more of a spiritual mentor, someone who encourages me to think more deeply about my faith. Laura and Heather, friends and coworkers who are part of my executive team, challenge me at work almost daily.

Each of these relationships is precious to me, and each one brings accountability, albeit in very different ways. They are the relationships that keep me grounded and keep me on track, the friendships that challenge me to be better and push me in the direction I want to go.

But accountability partnerships don't have to be limited to one-on-one relationships. You can also join or create your own accountability group, such as a business mastermind, exercise group, writing club, or Bible study. Accountability groups tend to be a little more formal, and they can be a great way to foster additional individual relationships with growth-minded people.

Just keep in mind that the key to creating any accountability partnership—whether it's a single person or a group—is finding people who are just as committed to the idea as you are, people who operate from a growth mind-set and genuinely want to see the same type of change and transformation happen in their own lives that you are looking to create in yours.

Here are some more tips for fostering true accountability in your relationships.

Dare to be vulnerable. Accountability doesn't work if you're on the defensive or if you're trying to present a polished version of yourself that doesn't accurately represent what you're feeling inside. And while that may still be the armor you present to the world at large, that shield needs to come down with the people you trust to hold you accountable.

Keep in mind too that it's especially easy to get defensive or to want to protect yourself or hide behind your mask when you're feeling stressed out or emotional or exhausted. Those are the times when accountability will feel the scariest, because even the gentlest feedback can feel like harsh criticism.

Good accountability partners will be able to see, at least eventually, when you are putting up that armor or hiding behind your normal defenses. Then they will encourage you to push past that instinct and get to the heart of the matter.

Set some ground rules. Not every accountability partnership needs to be formalized, but it's not a bad idea to establish some ground rules to make sure everyone is on the same page and comfortable with pushing back or with being pushed.

Ground rules for your Truth Club may include maintaining confidentiality (which should go without saying, but sometimes it does need to be said), as well as guidelines for when it's okay to give feedback and when it's time to just listen. Your ground rules may also include words or phrases to avoid, or perhaps even preferred methods of communication.

Get clear about your goals. It's hard to provide accountability if there aren't any goals or objectives to hold someone accountable to, so make sure the members of your Truth Club are very clear about sharing their goals and that you are diligent about keeping track of not only your own goals but your accountability partners' goals as well.

This may mean restating your goals whenever you meet or perhaps posting them someplace, such as in a shared Google Doc, Dropbox folder, or even a text thread.

Be intentional with your time. It's easy to get off track, as well as to avoid tough conversations, so to make the most of your accountability time, be sure to set some intentions at the beginning. What do you most want to get out of your time together? What are you struggling with that you would like help thinking through? Where do you need to be pushed? Where do you need to be encouraged?

Asking these types of questions can help set the tone, strip away pretense, and open up the conversation.

Check in regularly. For most of us, life can get pretty busy at times, and when things get crazy, it's almost always our relationships that suffer. So how will you make this accountability partnership a priority? You may want to set up a recurring appointment in your schedule or make a point of checking in once a week or once a month—whatever feels right.

My friend Bonnie and I always set our next lunch date before we say good-bye, because we know that if we don't, it will be months before it happens again. Likewise, with my Truth Club, we set a regular date and time for our monthly calls, and we schedule each of our three-day mastermind meetings several months in advance to make sure they're blocked out in everyone's schedule.

Ask questions and push back. The most important part of accountability is being able and willing to ask thoughtful and probing questions and to push back when necessary. This may mean calling someone out when they act in a way that's not in sync with their goals or beliefs. Or it may mean pushing someone forward when you see that their own limiting beliefs are holding them back.

This is where accountability can get uncomfortable, because it's the place where we move out of our comfort zone into uncharted territory. And that's a little scary, but it's also the point. Because everyone needs true accountability.

So go form your Truth Club. Do what it takes to discover your tribe, and then surround yourself with the people who will make you better and inspire you to take action. It may just be the most important thing you ever do.

chapter nineteen

stop comparing

Create the life you love, not the life someone else wants

Comparison is the thief of joy.	*Theodore Roosevelt*

It never fails.

Once a year, at the beginning of March, for five days only, we open up public enrollment for Elite Blog Academy and welcome in a new class of students who are ready to transform their passion into a full-time business. And in those first few weeks, the enthusiasm is off the charts. Everyone is starting in the exact same place, with the exact same assignment. Every incoming student is pumped up with the adrenaline of tackling something brand-new, while the alumni can't help but be reinvigorated by the energy. There is a sense of infinite possibility in the air.

It's so much fun!

But then, by about mid-April, the initial energy and excitement and enthusiasm start to wane. Because the reality is that building *any* sort of successful and profitable business is a lot of work, and growing an online business is no exception. Yes, the possibilities are infinite, but there's still a whole lot of effort involved. This is the point at which our students have to hunker down and actually do the work—their own work, on their own business, in their own time.

Most students figure this out, at least eventually. They begin to work their way through the lessons, one at a time, at their own pace, letting each unit build on the one before, the way the course is designed. They are the students who eventually succeed, though for some the journey is much longer than for others.

But there's always at least a handful of students who can't help but get caught up in what everyone else is doing. They start comparing their own ideas to others in the course, and they begin to doubt themselves. They notice that some people have moved through the lessons at a faster pace, and they start to believe that they are falling behind. Instead of focusing on their work and the clear path laid out for them in the course, they start looking for answers elsewhere—reading every new article that comes out on the topic of blogging, endlessly chatting in forums and Facebook groups, listening to dozens of podcasts, and taking multiple online courses all at once, all to ease the fear that they might be missing something.

And in the process of all this distraction, they get so much conflicting advice that they become practically paralyzed with indecision. They spend so much time looking at others around them that they can't focus on their own work.

Not surprisingly, these are the students who get stuck.

Because whether you're trying to build a business, manage your home, get promoted at work, or simply create a life you love, comparison is a giant trap that will suck you in and not let go.

And let's face it, it's hard to stay focused on your own path when there are so many opportunities to get distracted. Social media offers up a constant reminder of all the things we're *not* doing and all the things we may be missing out on. We compare jobs and clothes and cars and houses and status, not to mention parenting skills, social lives, and even relationships.

No matter how well we may be doing in one area, there's always someone else who seems to be doing it better or who is doing well in that area *plus* something else as well.

But just like those students in Elite Blog Academy, the more we look around to see what everyone else is doing and the more we compare our progress to that of those around us, the less success we will be able to create in our own lives and the less satisfied we will be.

Comparison breeds discontentment, and ultimately there's no way to win that game. Even so, there is a way to avoid the comparison trap that brings so many people down.

KNOW WHAT SUCCESS LOOKS LIKE TO YOU

I think the biggest reason comparison is so sinister is that it doesn't happen on an equal playing field. What you want, and what you view as success, is a destination that is unique to *you*. That means that often the people you're comparing yourself to are on a completely different journey—one with different rules and different objectives.

If your ultimate goal is not to have a home that looks like it belongs in a magazine or to drive a Cadillac Escalade, then what sense does it make to compare yourself—or your home or your vehicle—to the friend who has made that her primary objective? If you have no interest in climbing the corporate ladder and making a name for yourself in the business world, then why do you resent the sister-in-law who does have that interest? If traveling the world doesn't spark your passion, then why does it make you feel inadequate every time you hear about someone else's adventure?

Your journey is *your* journey, and ultimately creating a life you love means recognizing exactly what is most important and most meaningful to *you*. But it also means understanding that what is important and meaningful to you will not be the same as what is important and meaningful for other people, and vice versa. And that's okay.

You don't have to prove yourself to anyone but you.

What's more, you don't have to justify or explain your goals to anyone else or modify your own dreams to fit someone else's ideals. This is *your* journey. And if it works for you, then that's enough.

Of course, the key here is getting crystal clear about what *you* want and figuring out exactly what success looks like to you. Is it an amazing job that you're super passionate about? Plenty of free time to spend with your family or the ability to stay home with your kids? Is it being debt-free or paying off your mortgage? Is it a bigger house? A better car? Moving to a nicer neighborhood? Is it fostering deeper, more meaningful relationships with the people you care about most? Is it losing weight or getting in shape? Is it starting your own business? Is it selling everything you own, buying a boat, and sailing around the world? Or is it a passion for justice, for the alleviation of poverty, or for the environment? Or a desire to love and serve God?

What is it that *you* want most of all? What does creating a life you love look like for *you*, or for you and your spouse, or for you and your family? Because at the end of the day, *you* are the one who has to live it, and live *with* it.

That's why comparing yourself to anyone else is such a losing proposition. Because when you compare, you're comparing your path to someone else's road map. Which means the only possible result is getting lost.

So if you're going to avoid this comparison trap, the essential first step has to be to get completely clear about what you want most of all, as well as to get clear about your priorities and the path you will need to take.

Thankfully this is a process we've already talked about. You see, this happens when you claim your target and focus in on your big goal. It becomes even more solidified when you find your *why* and identify the deeper meaning behind that big goal. Your action plan, then, is your road map—the path you need to follow to get where you want to go.

PUT YOUR BLINDERS ON

And while we've already worked on creating that action plan, and while you may already have a road map to follow, the reality is that distractions are everywhere. Creating the plan is not the hard part; putting your head down, keeping your blinders on, trusting the plan, and actually doing the work—*that's* the hard part!

Taking action and following through without allowing yourself to be distracted or led astray is *always* the hard part. Because let's be real here—it's downright scary to put your faith in a plan that may not work. But I'll say it again: action is the antidote to fear. And the secret to success that so many people never realize is that as long as you keep taking small steps in one direction, you'll get there eventually.

The problem for most people is not that they chose the wrong path; instead, the problem for most people is that they keep leaping from path to path every time they hear a new idea or get swayed by what someone else is doing. And so rather than create momentum in one direction, they end up spinning in circles or moving back and forth, never actually getting anywhere.

It's exactly what happens to Elite Blog Academy students who spend all their time comparing their progress to others or picking and choosing what assignments they want to do or trying to do everything that everyone says, regardless of whether it's the right fit for where they happen to be at or where they want to go.

And it is exactly what happens with *any* goal when you're not willing to buckle down, put your blinders on, and do the work.

Think about it.

Let's say your biggest goal right now is to pay off your mortgage and credit cards and become 100 percent debt-free. And for a couple of months, you're doing *great*. You've stopped eating out, taken a break from shopping, and slashed your expenses every step of the way.

But then . . . life happens. You start seeing all the fun things your friends are posting on social media—vacations and new clothes and nights out on the town. You start to feel a little jealous. You start looking around a little more, and the big goal that felt so important and worthwhile starts to feel less so. You miss having fun. Slowly you start to slip back into your old ways. A Starbucks here, a new outfit there, the ever-more-regular date night at your favorite restaurant. Until one day you realize you're right back where you started.

Regardless of what you're aiming for, the same story plays out in a myriad of ways. There's the first initial period of enthusiasm and energy—the period that feels exciting and new. This is the part where you feel almost supercharged, like nothing can stand in your way. It's the initial burst of adrenaline that comes from stepping outside of your comfort zone. It feels exhilarating.

But it never lasts.

Because, you see, next comes the messy middle—the part where it gets real, and perhaps even painful. This is where the hard work happens, and it's the part that is often messy and frustrating and exhausting—but also totally necessary.

And *because* it's hard and *because* it's painful, this is also where people start looking around for something that feels easier or more fun and exciting. They compare where they're at right now—their messy middle—to someone else who has already done the work and made it to the other side, or they compare their situation to someone who's in the first stage of energy and enthusiasm, and they want to go back there.

Even if it means starting over with something new and never actually getting anywhere.

Depending on the goal, the messy middle stage can last a really, *really* long time. Weeks, months, even years. It takes determination, perseverance, and grit to make it through, as well as a willingness to put your blinders on, follow the plan, and just do the work that needs to be done.

The last phase is accomplishment—the part where you've done

the hard work, made an impact, and now reap the rewards of a job well done. Sadly, this is a phase not everyone gets to, because so many people get stuck or frustrated in the messy middle and decide to just keep starting over, again and again and again.

Don't let that be you.

Once you have your goal in front of you and your plan in place, put your blinders on. Stop looking around and stop comparing. Trust the process and understand that *it's supposed to be hard*. If it were easy, everyone would be doing it.

Remember, the greatest accomplishments are the ones you have to work for.

PRACTICE GRATITUDE

Of course, when it comes to staying out of the comparison trap, there's one more essential step that can make a tremendous difference, no matter what stage of the journey we happen to be in.

It's practicing gratitude.

Nothing is more humbling or perspective-giving than taking the time to think about the things you are grateful for.

In our everyday lives, comparison almost always leads to discontentment—a feeling that what we have or what we've accomplished or where we are at right now isn't enough. And while not all discontentment is bad—sometimes we need that gentle nudge to encourage us to face our fears or make a change—the angst that comes from feeling that what we have is lacking in comparison to someone else is generally not a good thing.

But gratitude turns that all around.

Instead of focusing on what we don't have, we focus on what we *do* have. Instead of beating ourselves up for what we haven't yet accomplished, we celebrate the little milestones along the way. Instead of only looking forward to what is still on the horizon, we also look back to acknowledge how far we've come.

We can't always control what happens to us or how other people treat us. But we do have control over how we decide to respond. And practicing a continual attitude of gratitude is the best way to avoid a victim mentality and to stop feeling like everyone else has got it better than we do.

And just as courage is a muscle that gets stronger every time you exercise it, so it is with gratitude—the more you practice it, the easier and more natural it comes, until it's just a part of you.

But the best part about practicing gratitude? It leads to instant happiness. Because it's pretty much impossible to feel discontentment when you're focused on the things you're grateful for.

Creating a life you *love* starts with appreciating the life you *have*. So stop comparing. Create the life you love, not the life someone else wants.

chapter twenty

eliminate excuses

Stop giving yourself a way out, and instead push through

I attribute my success to this: I never gave or took an excuse.	*Florence Nightingale, The Life of Florence Nightingale*

You would never know it, based on her level of perkiness and positivity, but my friend Susie was born with the deck stacked against her.

She grew up in poverty, on the UK's version of welfare, with a mom who suffered from mental illness and an alcoholic dad who regularly disappeared, sometimes for months or years at a time. As a result, her life was completely unpredictable.

Her family moved around all the time. In good times, they managed to find a place in the government-subsidized projects; in bad times, they stayed in homeless shelters. As a child, Susie was ashamed of a lot of things about her family, and she remembers trying to keep the details of her situation hidden from her teachers and classmates.

But then when she was a teenager, she stumbled across a book called *The Magic of Thinking Big*. In it was a chapter titled "No

Excuses," which explained that "excusitis" was the failure disease, and that if she wanted to succeed in life, she would need to cure herself of it forever. From that moment on, she vowed to live her life with no excuses and to refuse to let her circumstances define her.

And she didn't.

Despite having no formal education, she made her way first to Australia and then to the United States, where she built an incredibly successful career in corporate sales, working for a Fortune 500 company and earning a high-six-figure salary. And while most people would have been content there, Susie knew she was meant for something more, and she eventually walked away to start her own life coaching and motivational company.

Now the bestselling author of *What If It Does Work Out? How a Side Hustle Can Change Your Life*, Susie Moore inspires thousands of people to live their best lives, as she lives hers.[13]

All because she refused to make excuses.

Though her upbringing was set in Appalachia, a world away from the UK, my friend Edie's story followed a path similar to Susie's—a story she shares in heart-wrenching detail in her amazing memoir *All the Pretty Things*.[14] An alcoholic dad. Extreme poverty. Frequent hunger. No stability.

With no real role model to follow and a family of drunks, lunatics, and criminals surrounding her, Edie could have easily fallen into the same pattern. After all, it was all she knew. But, like Susie, Edie Wadsworth decided early on that she wasn't going to make excuses.

The defining moment for her happened when she was eight or nine years old and wanted to try out for a cheerleading team. At the time, her mom couldn't afford gymnastics lessons, so Edie would learn from the other girls on the playground who were taking gymnastics lessons, and she practiced so much that she got better than all of them. When cheerleading tryouts came, Edie knew she'd make the team because she could tumble better than anybody else.

And then, as she explained it, "I ended up not making the

squad, and the reason I didn't make it . . . I don't know if I was fully aware of this at the time, but I was that kid . . . You probably know a kid like this. They don't wear the right clothes. They look like they've not been quite taken care of in the right way. You look at them and go, oh, she has a good heart. I wish I could take her home. Well, I was that kid. I didn't have the right shoes. I didn't have the right clothes. I didn't come from the right family."[15]

A few other parents who had seen the tryouts were outraged when Edie didn't make the team, and they convinced the coach to change her mind. But when the coach stopped by the next day to offer her a spot, Edie's mom refused, telling the coach that she didn't deserve to have Edie on the team if she couldn't recognize her talent in the first place.

As Edie explains, "I remember in my own little child heart saying to myself, 'They will never be able to tell me no again. I will be so good. I will work harder than anybody. They will never be able to tell me no again.'"[16]

And from then on, Edie *did* work harder than anybody. She graduated with honors and went on to medical school and became a family physician. And then, much like Susie, she eventually left her established profession to start something of her own—first homeschooling her two youngest daughters and then eventually starting her own wildly successful business.

Both Susie and Edie could easily have let their disadvantages define their lives. And no one would have blamed them—they both would have been given a pass by society. After all, how could one possibly be expected to overcome such extreme poverty and dysfunction? It wasn't their fault. They were just victims of their circumstances.

But both Susie Moore and Edie Wadsworth refused to see themselves as victims, and they refused to give themselves an out. Their determination and drive to rise above their circumstances started with their conscious decision to stop making excuses.

Because truly, it's the only way.

KNOW THAT THE ONLY THING YOU CONTROL IS YOU

My kids go to a school that requires them to wear uniforms—a policy for which I am deeply grateful. You see, we had one year at a non-uniform school, and the daily battles over what to wear were enough to turn me into a pro-uniform evangelist forever!

But even with a relatively restrictive uniform policy in place, my daughter Maggie is still incredibly picky about what she wears. She reserves certain colors for certain days and takes a lot of pride in selecting the perfect hairbow, socks, and shoes to complement her look. And while at the start of the school year I ordered a few different skirt and skort options for her to rotate through, there is only one skirt she actually likes.

And so she wears it every day.

Normally this isn't a huge issue, because unlike Annie, who is generally a walking disaster, Maggie is not really a rough-and-tumble kid, which means her clothes stay pretty clean.

But one morning, my husband, Chuck—our resident breakfast chef extraordinaire—surprised us all with blueberry pancakes, a rare treat, especially on a weekday! We were all very excited, until Maggie cut into her last pancake and struck a particularly juicy blueberry, which practically exploded off the plate and onto her favorite skirt.

Disaster.

Almost instantly, what had been a surprisingly pleasant morning in the Soukup household devolved into a cacophony of wailing (Maggie), yelling (Chuck, who in addition to being head chef is also chief stain remover), singing (Annie, who was completely oblivious to and unaffected by the chaos unfolding around her), and laughing (me, at the ridiculousness of the entire situation).

Within minutes, it was clear that the skirt was not going to be wearable that day, which is where my previously sweet and perfectly pleasant daughter disappeared and the *real* drama began. There was crying and stomping and pouting and a whole lot of huffing, until finally I'd had enough.

In my best don't-mess-with-me mom voice, I told her she needed to pull herself together, that it was just a skirt and not the end of the world, considering that she had two other perfectly good—and practically brand-new—skirts available to wear.

And then, softening up just a little bit, I said, "Honey, there are always going to be things in life that happen outside of your control. And I'm sorry your skirt got ruined, but you still have a choice of whether you let this affect you. If you let this ruin your day, you are letting the blueberry win. Is that really what you want? To be defeated by a blueberry?"

It was a silly thing to say, but at least it elicited the briefest of smiles before the pouting began again.

But the truth is that there is so much in life that is outside of our control. We have no ability to predict the future or the weather or what major world events and catastrophes will occur. We don't get to pick our family of origin, the color of our skin, or our social and economic standing. We don't get to choose our IQ. At any given moment, we could experience an unexpected trauma, tragedy, illness, or setback—or yes, even a rogue blueberry that we never saw coming.

Indeed, the only sure thing about life is that it is completely and utterly unpredictable.

It's not so much a matter of *if* one of those things will happen, but *when*. Because they will happen. And that's why it's so critically important to understand, at the core of your being, that the only thing you will ever be able to control is *you*.

You can't control what happens to you or how people treat you, but you *can* control how you choose to respond. As we saw in chapter 10, your control is in the ownership you choose to take, regardless of the circumstances.

But make no mistake, taking full responsibility for your life can feel pretty scary. It means there is nothing left to hide behind and that you're standing out there in the open—vulnerable, exposed, and raw.

And that takes real courage.

LOOK FOR A ROLE MODEL, NOT A RESCUER

Jennifer Marx (whom I briefly mentioned in chapter 16) had been running her own travel guide business for twenty years before deciding it was time for something new. She was no stranger to hard work, but she was becoming more and more frustrated by an industry that was quickly becoming obsolete.

And so she sought guidance—someone who had been there and could show her the way. That's exactly what she found at Elite Blog Academy. In the spring of 2017, she dove into the course headfirst, put her blinders on, and completed every single assignment in order. Less than a year later, her new business venture and website, JenniferMaker.com, had far exceeded her travel business revenue.

When I asked her what she attributed her success to in EBA, she explained that although she had been in business for many years, she had never had a role model before, someone who had been there and who could show her what was possible. And when she finally saw what was possible, she realized that she could do it too.

It's only natural when facing the unknown, trying to do something you've never done before, or feeling unsure to look for a role model or someone else to guide you along the way. Because let's face it, in any endeavor in life, it's nice to have someone who has been there, who gets it, and who knows exactly what you're going through. It's helpful to have someone willing to offer their wisdom and advice and maybe even to show you exactly what to do.

And that's true no matter what you may be going through. Nothing is more reassuring to a new mom than another mom who offers firsthand advice on everything from feeding to teething to sleeping through the night. Nothing is more helpful to an entrepreneur than talking or listening to other, more experienced business owners.

Indeed, in many professions, the importance of mentorship and guidance is built right in. Professional athletes have coaches. Doctors start as interns and then become residents under the guidance of more experienced attending physicians. Lawyers start as associates or clerks before moving up the chain.

No one wants to feel like they're going it alone, wading into uncharted territory all by themselves. It's comforting to be able to follow in someone else's footsteps and reassuring to know that whatever you're trying to do *is* actually possible because someone else has done it.

In general, role models, teachers, mentors, and coaches are a good thing, especially when it comes to doing it scared. And so, if you're preparing to break out of your comfort zone and try something new, finding someone to guide you along the way can be a really smart idea. That person can help you avoid pitfalls and let you know you're on the right track. It may mean taking a class or hiring a coach, or just talking to someone who has already done the thing that you want to do.

But there's a catch.

You see, a role model is someone *you* seek out for guidance, not the other way around. And that's a very different scenario from simply hoping for someone else to figure it out for you or show you the way. Looking for a role model is not the same thing as waiting to be rescued.

And it is crucial to understand the difference.

When you actively seek out a role model for guidance, you assume responsibility and take ownership of your journey. You are proactive, not reactive, and you understand that the job of your role model is not to do the work for you, but to show you that it can be done and to offer guidance along the way.

When all you do is wait for a rescuer or sit around wishing and hoping that someone will help make things easier, you're allowing yourself to be the victim. What's worse, you are giving away all your power to someone who may or may not ever show up.

When Jennifer Marx signed up for Elite Blog Academy, the biggest thing she got was a clear path to the result she wanted. But she was still the one who had to take ownership of that path, and *she* was the one who had to do the work.

I guarantee that you do *not* need to be rescued, but you may need a role model. Fortunately for you, there are role models, teachers, coaches, and mentors everywhere you look; you just have to start looking. They will help you eliminate excuses and encourage you to push through the tough times.

HOW TO FIND A MENTOR

Over the past several years, I've had a number of different mentors, both formal and informal, who have helped me in both my business and in life, and I enjoy getting to be a mentor to others as well.

What I've learned is that there's something incredibly powerful about getting the perspective of someone who has more experience than you, whether it's in life or in business. It stretches you in a way you'll never be stretched all on your own, and ultimately, that is almost always a good thing.

Why Have a Mentor?

Mentors will support your growth and can teach you things you'd never learn if you only interacted with your peers. You may think you're getting great perspective from those in your current circle, but if you never step outside that circle, I guarantee you are missing something.

Now the great thing is, a mentor doesn't have to be someone you have coffee with once a week. Your mentor can be someone who inspires you through books, podcasts, or a blog.

What to Look For in a Mentor

Sadly, there are lots of people out there claiming to be mentors, experts, and business or life coaches who have no business giving advice. Sometimes it's because they don't have any real experience; other times it's because they're good at promoting themselves, but they're not skilled at teaching and mentoring others to do the same.

If you're going to look for a mentor, I recommend that you pay close attention, first of all, to the kind of success the person has created in their own life or business. Is that person seeing the kind of results you would like to see? Are they financially solvent? Is their personal life strong? It's okay to ask these questions and to ask for transparency—especially if you're hiring someone to be a mentor.

And here's a strong warning: Don't take business advice from someone who doesn't have actual business experience. This goes for someone you're paying to mentor you, obviously, but also for anyone who is handing out free advice. Be careful about who you listen to, and feel free to ignore *anyone*—no matter how confident or authoritative they may appear—who isn't getting real results.

The second thing to look for is that the mentor is someone you can actually learn from—someone whose teaching style and advice resonate with you. Our brains all work a little differently, which means the way some people talk or teach will really connect with you, while the way others talk or teach just won't. And that's okay.

And finally, look for recommendations. Ask for referrals from other people in your space, and don't be afraid to ask a potential mentor if they have any references you can talk to.

Are You Ready to Be Mentored?

While it's perfectly okay to start out with "virtual" mentors who teach from afar, there will come a point when you'll want to consider paying for a coach or mentor. The reality is that when you pay for something, you tend to value it a whole lot more, which means you'll take their advice much more seriously, be more likely to implement suggestions, and ultimately get better results. Free advice just doesn't hold the same weight.

If you feel like a more personal mentor is an essential part of your growth, go for it! Try a formalized coaching program or a mastermind group. It's a great way to get the individualized attention you need and grow exponentially in the process.

Whether you find a virtual mentor to teach you from afar or a more individualized mentor to work with you one-on-one, working with a mentor can push you to a level you've never dreamed of. And you deserve that kind of support.

EVEN A GOOD EXCUSE IS STILL AN EXCUSE

We all know those people—the ones who always have some sort of excuse or justification, some reason why it's not their fault, some explanation that gets them off the hook. Some magical way of shifting the blame away from themselves.

Maybe you are that person.

After all, excuses are never in short supply. My husband often jokes that women can justify and rationalize almost anything, but quite honestly, I don't think women are the only ones who can do that. I think everyone can. It's not too hard to come up with equally good reasons why or why not.

If you're looking for an excuse, you will always be able to find one. But remember, even a good excuse is still just an excuse. The only way to escape the disease of excusitis is to refuse to make it an option under any circumstances.

At any point in their lives, both Susie and Edie could have selected from any number of perfectly legitimate and reasonable excuses. Growing up in poverty. A dysfunctional family. Addiction. Abuse. Lack of opportunity. No guidance along the way.

And not one single person would have blamed either of them for not rising above it all, for not making anything of their lives. How could they? They were clearly victims of an unfair system. How could they possibly be expected to overcome all those disadvantages?

And yet they both did.

Which means you can too.

But it starts with refusing to make excuses, no matter what.

From here on out, eliminate excuses from your vocabulary. Stop looking for justification—because you'll always find it—and instead focus on the one thing you can control, namely, *yourself.* Stop looking for a rescuer, and instead actively pursue a role model to follow.

Stop giving yourself a way out, and instead push through.

chapter twenty-one

stay encouraged

Take the time to celebrate your wins along the way

| In the middle of every difficulty lies opportunity. | *Albert Einstein* |

Let's not kid ourselves here. Doing it scared is not for the faint of heart. The process of facing our fears and going after big goals and dreams is not always easy. In fact, it very rarely is.

After all, if it were easy, everyone would be doing it. If it were easy, it wouldn't be special or significant or noteworthy. If it were easy, it wouldn't be worth fighting for.

And while on one level, in theory, most of us probably understand that doing it scared is hard, on a practical level, it's not always easy to remember. When things get hard or disappointments and obstacles show up, all the optimism and excitement we felt in the beginning is soon replaced with discouragement, frustration, and fear.

We don't want it to be hard. We don't want it to hurt. We don't want to get our hands dirty or have to fight for what we want or feel the pain of defeat or the humiliation of failure. We don't want to face adversity or risk being judged by others. We don't want to have to take responsibility or find out we might not be good enough to achieve what we want.

When the going gets tough, it can be tough to stay encouraged. But that's exactly the time when you need encouragement the most. And while you could sit around waiting and wishing and hoping for that encouragement to come from somewhere or someone else, the reality is that you'll probably be waiting a very long time.

Remember, in the end, the only thing you can ever control is you—not what happens to you, but *how you choose to respond*. And that means that one of the very best things you can do for yourself is learn how to put safeguards in place that will help you avoid and overcome discouragement and find more joy along the way.

BEWARE OF THE SPACE BETWEEN

For each of the last couple of years, I've had the honor of coaching a small group of women entrepreneurs in a private business mastermind. It's pretty intense, and over the course of our year together, I've enjoyed watching the personal and business growth that happens. And while technically I am the teacher, I feel like I always learn far more than I teach.

While I do have a fairly rigorous application process for joining the mastermind, I don't select the members based on the size, scope, or focus of their business. Instead, I'm always looking for the people with the best potential—the ones whose mind-set and attitude indicate that they are willing to do the work, even if they're starting at the beginning. And because everyone in the group shares a similar growth mind-set, most of the time it doesn't seem to matter that they each have very different businesses.

But that doesn't mean comparison never happens.

Not long ago, during one of our monthly calls, one of my members, Nicole, shared with the group that she was feeling incredibly discouraged. She had been working so hard, doing all the things we had identified for her as priorities at our last workshop, but she didn't feel like things were happening fast enough. She still felt like she was lagging behind.

Now, Nicole had applied to be in this mastermind, even though she was just getting started—her baby business had been up and running for less than a year. She was driven to succeed, and she figured there would be no better way to start out on the right foot than with a strong group of women who had already been there and could show her the way.

And in many ways, she was exactly right. Because of the advice she was receiving in this group, she would be able to significantly shorten her learning curve and grow her business much, much faster.

But as I warned her at the beginning, just because she was in the group, success wouldn't happen for her overnight. In our first one-on-one session, I explained that her biggest danger was not that she wasn't ready for this mastermind, but that she could get caught in the trap of comparing where she was right now—still building her foundation—to where other members of the group might be.

"Nicole, you're going to have to fight to own your own journey. There will be times when it seems like everyone else gets to focus on things that are more exciting than where you're at right now. You get the benefit of seeing what's possible, and that is going to be huge for you. But if you don't build your foundation, you'll never be able to get there."

She promised me that she understood. And I know she did. But when all the day-to-day stuff happens, when things start to feel hard, it's only human nature to forget those kinds of warnings. In fact, that's exactly why it's so helpful to have a coach or mentor to remind you.

So when Nicole showed up to our group conference call feeling discouraged and frustrated, I gently reminded her that this was exactly the stage she needed to be in right now. And then I asked her an important question.

"How often are you looking back to see how far you've come versus looking forward to see how far you still have to go?"

Nicole thought about it for a while before answering. "I'm not really looking back at all," she admitted. "I just keep seeing all the places I want to go."

You could almost see the lightbulb go on, and it was, as she says, a moment that changed her. She actually felt her perspective shift.

From then on, she began keeping a "Success Log," a simple spreadsheet designed to record all her wins. And every single day, she documents at least one triumph or success, however small. That one simple act, repeated every day, has changed everything for Nicole. Instead of feeling frustrated at her lack of progress, she is constantly reminded of how far she has come.

When it comes to creating a life we love, those big goals that we identify and commit to are *key*. They are the catalysts that light a fire in our belly, that make our chest tighten and get us motivated to do more and be more than we ever thought we were capable of. They give us something to strive for and a reason to jump out of bed in the morning.

But as important as they are, those big goals also pose a danger.

Have you ever noticed when driving on a hot, sunny day that it sometimes looks like there's a shiny wet spot up ahead? It's known as a highway mirage, and according to Wikipedia, it happens because "convection causes the temperature of the air to vary, and the variation between the hot air at the surface of the road and the denser cool air above it creates a gradient in the refractive index of the air."[17]

The most infuriating thing about this mirage is that you can never actually get to it. No matter how long or how far you drive, it's always somewhere up ahead, far off in the distance.

Unfortunately our big goals can sometimes start to feel exactly like that highway mirage—always just out of reach. Instead of motivating us, they become a source of frustration and discouragement because they seem so far away. And when that messy middle hits and things start to get hard and painful and intense, it's only natural to feel discouraged or convinced you'll never get there.

It is all too easy to fall into "the space between," that place somewhere in the middle of where you are and where you want to be. It's that place where you have all these big goals and there's always more to do to get there, but you never quite make it.

If we spend all our time in this space between, we'll never feel like we're getting anywhere or accomplishing anything, even though we actually are. That's why it's so important to take time each day to look back instead of only looking forward, to celebrate your wins and accomplishments rather than continuously focusing on all the things you haven't done just yet.

Having clear goals is wonderful, and being a goal-oriented person can be a huge strength, but neglecting to focus on what you've already accomplished and what you're continuing to accomplish—even if you aren't quite there yet—can easily bring you down.

In the end, you need to find the joy in the journey, not just the destination. And the only way to do that is to stay out of the space between. Yes, dare to look ahead and see what's possible. But also remember to look back and take stock of how far you've come.

CHANGE THE SCRIPT

Not too long ago, I was chatting with my friend Kyle about writing, and he said, "I'd really like to focus on my blog, but I've got some major insecurities when it comes to writing. My fifth-grade teacher told me I wasn't a good writer, and whenever I sit down to write, it's her voice I hear in my head. I think that's what has always held me back."

And right away, I spotted it. Do you see it too?

It was a limiting belief—a belief that was holding him back from achieving his full potential.

Of course, my friend Kyle is not the only one with limiting beliefs about what he is capable of. He's not the only one with that little voice in his head telling him he can't do something.

We all have that voice.

It may be telling us we don't deserve to ask for that raise, or it may be saying we aren't as talented or witty or well-spoken as a coworker. It may be whispering things such as, "You're not a good mom," or "You're a terrible housekeeper," or "You'll never get organized," or "You totally suck at math." It could be telling us we can't actually become debt-free or saying we're not smart enough to be successful. It could be saying we're too busy to go after our big goals and dreams or that we don't have time to read or learn or do something for ourselves.

That voice may be warning us not to try new things or take a risk because we might fail. Or the warning may be that we don't want to reach out and ask for help because we might get rejected. It could be telling us not to put 100 percent of our energy and effort into pursuing our dreams because we're not sure what the people around us will say. "What if they don't understand," it whispers, "or what if they make fun of me?"

Whatever your voice is saying, and whatever your limiting beliefs may be, I guarantee they are there. And while we can't always stop those limiting beliefs from popping up or that voice from whispering in our ear, we *can* refuse to pay attention to them!

The reason our limiting beliefs have so much power over us is that we don't realize that what we are hearing inside of our heads isn't necessarily based on truth but is based on fear.

We just assume that the message we're hearing—the voice, the thought, the limiting belief—is our reality, when the truth is that it is nothing more than just that: a voice or a thought or a limiting belief. Just because the voice in our head is telling us that something is true doesn't mean it actually *is* true. In fact, often—almost always, I dare say—it's not *at all* true.

It's just a thought.

But when we name the fear that is behind the limiting belief or the voice in our head, once we've recognized a limiting belief for what it is—just a thought that is holding us back—we can take away the power it has over us and move past it. That's when we can say, "That voice in my head is telling me I'm not smart enough to be successful, but really it's that I'm afraid of making a mistake. But even smart people make mistakes, and that is how they learn."

It's called changing the script. You know—the self-talk message that's stuck playing in your head on repeat. The one that keeps telling you that you're not good enough or smart enough or pretty enough, or that you'll never succeed or never get organized or can't write or shouldn't even bother trying.

It's the script that keeps telling you that you can't.

If you want to stop listening to that message, you need to figure out some way of replacing it with a new message.

Think about it. If the self-talk currently going on in your head is programming your brain to believe things about yourself that are untrue, then the best way to reprogram your brain is to start replacing the negative self-talk messages with something new. Something that actually *is* true.

We have to start changing the message being played into something that is not so self-defeating. For my friend Kyle, it may mean replacing the tape inside his head that's telling him he can't write. What do you think would happen if every day, maybe even several times a day, Kyle started saying something to himself such as, "The more I write, the better writer I will become. It takes time and practice to hone a craft, and I can keep practicing indefinitely. Just because one person, a long time ago, didn't like my writing doesn't mean I don't have something valuable to say. There have been many other people who have liked and appreciated my writing, and so I will keep writing and keep improving so I can make an impact with my words."

It may take a little while, but his brain and his subconscious will start to accept this new message as his new truth, and the limiting belief that tells him he isn't a good writer will start to fade away.

But also notice what the new message *doesn't* say. It doesn't say, "I'm the best writer the world has ever seen. I am a rock star. No one can write as well as I can." That message wouldn't resonate, because Kyle wouldn't believe it to be true.

Instead, the new message needs to take whatever message is currently playing and reframe it in a different, more positive, but very specific way. And it needs to be scripted with honesty, so that you can reset your truth and actually begin to believe and internalize the new message.

Change the script and you will change your outlook, guaranteed.

KEEP FILLING UP

As humans, we have an insatiable need for encouragement. It doesn't seem to matter how often we hear that we're smart or capable or beautiful or courageous or any other number of positive messages, we still need to hear it again and again. No sooner than we've heard it, we forget it again. Life gets crazy or hard or stressful; self-doubt and all those fears creep in. And suddenly our confidence starts to fade away yet again.

That's why it's so important to *keep filling up*. There is no limit to the number of motivational and self-help books you should read, the number of times you should read your favorite Bible verses or devotionals, the number of inspirational podcasts you should listen to, or the number of events or gatherings you should attend, because the energy and excitement, the motivation and the inspiration that feel so incredible in the moment, will eventually fade away. But even so, the more positive and uplifting messages you have pouring in, the more likely you'll be to hold on to some of it.

You need to keep filling up.

Make it a habit to listen to podcasts while you're driving or working out or doing the dishes. (The *Do It Scared* podcast is a great one to start with!) Make it a goal to read at least one inspiring book a month, or just read your favorites over and over. Be on the lookout for events and gatherings in your area that will get you fired up and allow you to meet like-minded people. Schedule time with the friends and mentors who you know will both challenge and encourage you.

Actively work at staying motivated, and make encouragement and inspiration a priority so the progress you make doesn't fade away.

PRACTICE SELF-CARE

A couple of years ago, I did something I'd never done before—something I don't think I ever would have even considered, had my husband not suggested and encouraged it.

I went on a personal retreat.

For four whole days, I did nothing but read books, journal, go for long walks and hikes, do yoga, take leisurely baths, and lie by the pool. I completely unplugged from work and literally retreated from the world. And I slept. A lot.

I came back to my family—and my work—completely recharged, revitalized, and reinvigorated. I don't think even I had realized how close I was to burnout until I went, but those four days alone were nothing short of amazing. It was a powerful reminder to me—someone who normally thrives on being busy—that sometimes rest is the most productive thing we can do.

In fact, in the years since, I've become vigilant about scheduling intentional downtime and personal retreats at least every couple of months. As an introvert who spends a lot of time doing extroverted activities, alone time is the only surefire way to recharge my batteries.

And yet a few months ago, when I posted a picture on social media from one of these retreats, I was shocked by the number of women who responded with comments such as, "Sounds lovely, but I could never do that," or "Wow, I so wish I could go on a retreat, but it's impossible."

Let me just tell you, it's not impossible. Your "retreat" doesn't have to be an elaborate vacation at a five-star resort. Some of my best retreats have been at home when my husband has taken our kids camping for the weekend. Your retreat also doesn't have to be alone! For me, alone time is restorative, but for an extrovert who is feeling isolated, a weekend with friends can be what fills your soul.

The point is not what you do to take care of yourself, but that you actually *do* make time for yourself without feeling guilty about it.

Because the truth is that taking the time to take care of *you* is better for everyone. Obviously there's the immediate benefit—you have fun and get to do what you want in the moment. You feel happy. You relax and smile. But longer term, the stress of neglecting your own needs has very negative effects on your body, mind, and soul.

When we feel stretched too thin, we're unable to give 100 percent to anyone or anything. Allowing ourselves a little "me time" every now and then is like a release valve for all the pressure that builds up. It results in more energy and less exhaustion, helps boost our immune system, and makes us feel calmer, kinder, and more in control of our emotions.

Moreover, taking time to care for our own well-being restores our ability to care for the other people in our life—our spouse, kids, friends, and extended family. The people closest to us tend to bear the brunt of our stress, which means they also stand to benefit the most from our self-care.

While it may feel selfish or indulgent in the moment—especially if you've never done it before—it's not. Remember the oxygen-mask-on-an-airplane principle? When you adjust your own mask before assisting others, your act of self-care is actually one of the *least* selfish things you can do.

CELEBRATE EVERY WIN

Courage is a daily decision—one that requires the willingness to act, even in the face of fear, and to keep taking steps toward your goals, even when you're not always sure where the path is going to lead.

But even as you push toward your goals, it's easy to forget how far you've come, which is why it's so important to make sure you are not only looking forward but also looking back. So document your success. Keep a gratitude journal or a success log, and take the time to celebrate your wins along the way. Create new self-talk scripts that motivate you with truth and honesty. Take care of yourself. And stay encouraged.

In the end, remember that this book is not intended to be a passive read, but one that spurs you to take action in your own life. If you haven't already, I strongly encourage you to take advantage of our resources and the Do It Scared Fear Assessment at doitscared. com. There you'll find tools that can help you take the next step in your journey and apply the lessons found here.

Because you are stronger than you think you are. You *can* do it, and you can do it scared. And when you keep going no matter what, you'll get one step closer to creating a life you love.

courage in action at a glance

1. CLAIM YOUR TARGET
If you aim at nothing, you'll hit it every time. Get clear about your big goal, and narrow your focus to stay pointed in the right direction.

2. FIND YOUR *WHY*
Your *why* must be bigger than your fear, so make sure you know exactly why this particular goal matters to you, and create a catalyst to help you stay motivated.

3. CREATE YOUR ACTION PLAN
Break down your big goals into manageable bites and then make the daily decision to follow through and actually get one step closer to your goal.

4. FORM YOUR OWN TRUTH CLUB
Seek out accountability in your life and actively surround yourself with people who will speak truth to you, help push you past your fears, and ultimately make you better.

5. STOP COMPARING

Accept full responsibility for the choices you make and for the goals you want to pursue. Then put your blinders on and create the life you love, not the life someone else wants.

6. ELIMINATE EXCUSES

Refuse to make excuses for anything in your life, because even a good excuse is still an excuse. Stop giving yourself a way out, and instead choose to push through.

7. STAY ENCOURAGED

Put safeguards in place that will keep you motivated. Take the time to celebrate your wins along the way, and remember to practice self-care.

acknowledgments

This book would not have been possible without the help and guidance of the following people. Thank you for your impact on my life, my work, and this book.

Chuck, my rock, my love, and my best friend. Thank you for supporting me and cheering me on, no matter what. Thank you for encouraging me when I feel like quitting, challenging me when I need to be pushed, making me laugh, and always reminding me to take my own advice and do it scared.

Maggie and Annie, my sweet girls. I love you so much, and I'm so proud of both of you. Thank you for always giving me something to write about. You keep me humble and remind me of what matters most.

My RSO family—Laura, Heather, Jayson, Natalie, Jessica, Kelly, Kristene, Emma, Melissa, Amanda, Maggie, LaTrisha, Ashley, and Danny. Thank you for making it a joy to come to work every day. Thank you for being all in, supporting my crazy ideas, telling me no when necessary, and forcing me to sit down and WRITE (even when I didn't want to!). I love our constructive conflict, our L10s, and our daily huddles, and I love the way you always push me to be better. Seriously, how lucky am I that I get to work with each and every one of you each day?

Friends I adore, both old and new, who provide much-needed accountability, encouragement, and tough love—Alysha, Edie, Bonnie, Heather, Laura, Natalie, Kate, Susie, Gry, Laura, Janna, Shelly, Bill and Wendy, Lisa, Melissa, Rachel—I'm so grateful for each and every one of you!

Grant and your whole team at Launch Thought Productions, for helping us sift through all the research and then helping us conceptualize and build the Fear Assessment. This amazing tool would not exist without your team!

Lori, for both your patience and your pushiness. I am so thankful to have been able to work with you again on another book!

Charles and Meg, for always keeping our books in order, Bond for always helping us crush our goals, and Full Cycle Marketing for being such a big part of this Do It Scared journey.

All the people who helped bring this book to life and get it out there to the world—the whole Zondervan team, especially Carolyn, Alicia, and Dirk; Andrew Wolgemuth, my literary agent; and Ashley Bernardi, the best publicist ever!

And last but definitely not least—all the blog readers, podcast listeners, planner customers, and EBA students who make our incredible community what it is. Your passion, courage, and compassion inspire me every single day! I love watching you do it scared, and then encouraging others to do the same. Together we can change the world!

notes

1. See Stanley Milgram, *Obedience to Authority: An Experimental View* (New York: Harper & Row, 1974).
2. Charles Duhigg, *Smarter, Faster, Better: The Transformative Power of Real Productivity* (New York: Random House, 2017), 31.
3. Jocko Willink and Leif Babin, *Extreme Ownership: How U.S. Seals Lead and Win* (New York: St. Martin's, 2015), 30–31.
4. See Helen Weathers, "Griffiths Lottery Win," *Daily Mail*, March 22, 2013, www.dailymail.co.uk/news/article-2297798/ Griffiths-lottery-win-How-winning-1-8m-wreck-life.html.
5. See Teresa Dixon Murray, "Why Do 70 Percent of Lottery Winners End Up Bankrupt?" *Plain Dealer*, January 14, 2016, www.cleveland.com/business/index.ssf/2016/01/why_do _70_percent_of_lottery_w.html.
6. See Jimmy Evans and Allan Kelsey, *Strengths Based Marriage: Build a Stronger Relationship by Understanding Each Other's Gifts* (Nashville: Nelson, 2016).
7. Patrick Lencioni, *The Five Dysfunctions of a Team: A Leadership Fable* (San Francisco: Jossey-Bass, 2002).
8. See Brigid Schulte, "Making Time for Kids? Study Says Quality Trumps Quantity," *Washington Post*, March 28, 2015, www.washingtonpost.com/local/making-time-for-kids-study

-says-quality-trumps-quantity/2015/03/28/10813192-d378
-11e4-8fce-3941fc548f1c_story.html.

9. Angela Duckworth, *Grit: The Power of Passion and Perseverance* (New York: Simon & Schuster, 2016).

10. Carol Dweck, *Mindset: The New Psychology of Success* (New York: Ballantine, 2006), 6.

11. Brian Tracy, *Eat That Frog: 21 Great Ways to Stop Procrastinating and Get More Done in Less Time* (San Francisco: Berrett-Koehler, 2001), 2.

12. Cited in Leo Widrich, "How the People around You Affect Personal Success," Lifehacker, July 16, 2012, https://life hacker.com/5926309/how-the-people-around-you-affect -personal-success.

13. Susie Moore, *What If It Does Work Out? How a Side Hustle Can Change Your Life* (Mineola, NY: Ixia, 2016).

14. Edie Wadsworth, *All the Pretty Things: The Story of a Southern Girl Who Went through Fire to Find Her Way Home* (Carol Stream, IL: Tyndale, 2016).

15. "Perseverance, Determination, and Living Your Best Life: An Interview with Edie Wadsworth," transcript of episode 10, *Do It Scared with Ruth Soukup* podcast, https://doitscared .com/episode10.

16. "Perseverance, Determination, and Living Your Best Life."

17. "Mirage," Wikipedia, https://en.wikipedia.org/wiki/Mirage.